Presented to

_____

On the occasion of

_____

From

_____

Date

_____

GOD'S WORD FOR

SIMPLE
ABUNDANCE

Dan & Nancy Dick

BARBOUR
PUBLISHING, INC.
Uhrichsville, Ohio

INTRODUCTION

God's Word offers the perfect antidote to the high-speed, stressed-out lifestyle of our modern society. In the pages of the Bible you'll find the key to slowing down, simplifying your life, and enjoying God's presence. You'll learn how to better relate to the people and circumstances that come into your life. You'll discover the pathway to a simple abundance.

This book, *God's Word for Simple Abundance,* will guide you along the way. Six months' worth of devotions (180 in all) will lead you through the ancient yet timely biblical book of Proverbs, mining its wisdom and offering insights for your life today.

These devotions will lead you on an inspirational journey to spiritual maturity in your relationship with Jesus Christ. If you have never accepted Jesus Christ as the Son of God—and the personal Savior of those who receive Him—take time to read a few Bible verses (John 3:3, John 3:16, Romans 6:23, Romans 10:9) before you start this book. More than anything else, this decision will lead you to a life of peace and joy.

Commit to time with God, in His Word, for the next few months, and you'll be amazed at the difference it can make in your life. Read on to experience *God's Word for Simple Abundance.*

BE YE PERFECT

The proverbs of Solomon the son of David, King of Israel:
to know wisdom and instruction;
to perceive the words of understanding.
PROVERBS 1:1–2

There is no easy way to be a Christian. Christianity requires a lot of effort, sacrifice, and commitment. The heart of the Christian life is to love the way Christ taught and lived. Though it sounds simple, it is terribly difficult. The temptation is to throw up our hands and say, "I'm not Christ! I can't do the things He did!" Still, Christ Himself said that we should "Be. . .perfect, even as your Father which is in heaven is perfect" (Matthew 5:48). How can Christ ask such a thing of us?

Christ never for one minute thought that we would be perfect as God is. He knows that we are imperfect and sinful. He also knows how much God loves us and wants us to grow and to be happy. With His help, we can find joy and maturity. To assist us, God gave His Word, the Holy Scriptures. If we will be dedicated to reading the Bible regularly and do it prayerfully, God will help us to understand it; and through understanding, we will be able to live more perfectly, the way God intends.

PRAYER: O Lord, help me to know You, and through knowing You, help me to be like You. Make me a faithful and loving follower, and be with me to guide me this day, and every day to come. Amen.

EXPERIENCE—THE BEST TEACHER

The proverbs of Solomon the son of David, king of Israel. . .
To give subtilty to the simple,
to the young man knowledge and discretion.
PROVERBS 1:1, 4

The saying is certainly true which says, "Experience is the best teacher." It is through day-to-day living that we come to understand life. What we did not understand as children, we come to know as adults. When we start upon a new endeavor, we learn slowly, gathering more information and experience, until we finally master it.

Our Christian life is like that. We start out inexperienced and with little knowledge, but then we grow in our understanding and commitment. Christ Himself spent a good deal of His life preparing for His ministry and work. Like Him, we are growing, maturing, and preparing for the Kingdom of God which awaits us. When we search for God in the Bible and through prayer, we are being made ready for our heavenly home. In this life, we never really arrive at "being" Christian, but we are ever "becoming" Christian. As long as we continue to learn, we continue to grow. In that growth lies wisdom.

PRAYER: Dear heavenly Father, grant that I might continue to learn more about You each and every day. Create in me a real hunger for Your truth. Amen.

THE FEAR OF THE LORD

The fear of the LORD is the beginning of knowledge:
but fools despise wisdom and instruction.
PROVERBS 1:7

Standing on the shore of a great ocean, one is amazed at the force of the waves crashing on the rocks. The vast expanse of water is awe-inspiring, yet it is beautiful. Only a very foolish person would ignore the dangers presented by the sea, yet only a fool would not be attracted by its beauty. The ocean is to be feared and respected, but it is also to be experienced. Despite our sense of awe, or perhaps because of it, we are drawn to the water, to be immersed in it, to become part of it. Our true enjoyment of the surf comes when we enter in, but only when we understand its power.

The same is true of God. We stand in awe before Him, wisely cautious in the face of His power; yet we long to know Him, to be united with Him. The wise pursue Him with all their heart, while the foolish ignore Him or reject Him because of their fear. Once we understand the power of our Lord, this fear enables us to be with Him, immersed in Him, but always respecting His might.

PRAYER: O Lord, help me to know fear in a positive way, and set my feet on the path to wisdom. Amen.

TEMPTATION

My son, if sinners entice thee, consent thou not.
PROVERBS 1:10

Our Lord, Jesus Christ, once walked in the wilderness. He fasted forty days, and when it was past, Satan came and walked with Him. Christ, hungry as He was, refused to be tempted by Satan's charge to turn some stones into bread. Christ, poor as He was by worldly standards, withstood the allure of wealth, fame, and power. Christ, holy as He was, refused to put God to a test. In the face of enormous enticement, Jesus stood firmly consenting to none of Satan's requests.

It sounds so easy, "consent thou not." Yet many desirable things tempt us. How are we to resist the multitude of temptations we face every day? We resist temptation the same way Jesus did—with the help of the Holy Spirit.

As we grow in our knowledge of God, we feel His presence in our lives, and we become able to rely on His strength to resist enticement when our strength is not enough. Our choice is whether or not we will allow God to strengthen us when we need it most.

PRAYER: O Lord, be with me in the face of temptation. Grant me the wisdom and courage I need to resist enticement, and help me turn to Thee. Amen.

GIVING VS. GREED

So are the ways of every one that is greedy of gain;
which taketh away the life of the owners thereof.
PROVERBS 1:19

An important question each person should ask is, "How much do I really need?" Christ is quite clear about the accumulation of wealth. As in the story of the man who built his storehouses bigger to hold his great crops, Christ also asks each one of us where it is we keep our treasure. Is it on earth, or is it in heaven? Surely God wants every person to enjoy life and to share in good times, but He does not find joy in the celebration of a few when many suffer.

A good guideline to follow concerning the possessions of this world is to contemplate the question of what Christ might do with the same possessions if they were His. If this rule were followed, much more would be given and shared, and fewer people would have to do without. The Bible says that greed is keeping what we don't need. God rejoices in the life of a giver but has no part of the greedy person's life. With His help and guidance, we all can learn to be more giving.

PRAYER: O heavenly Father, open my eyes to the needs of those around me. Destroy the spirit of selfishness in my heart, and teach me to give as You would give. Amen.

GOD'S RULES

Turn you at my reproof:
behold, I will pour out my spirit unto you,
I will make known my words unto you.
PROVERBS 1:23

A young woman remembered her girlhood with mixed feelings. When she had been younger, she had resisted every effort her parents had made to impose rules on her. She resented the fact that her mother and father continually told her what to do. Her usual response was, "When I have children of my own, I'll never treat them the way you treat me."

When she did, in fact, have children of her own, the words came back to haunt her. She began to understand better why her parents had acted as they had. She began to see the wisdom in her parents' actions and words. Her eyes were opened to the true intentions of her parents: to try to do what was best for their daughter.

The rules and laws of God often have the same effect on us. We resist them, thinking that God doesn't want us to have any fun. If we will only realize that every rule God gives is given out of perfect love for us, we can truly enjoy our lives the way God intends us to. By obeying, we learn more about God.

PRAYER: Dear God, help me to be obedient to Your will. Please help me not to question Your wisdom but to always trust You. If I do, understanding will follow. Amen.

INCLUDING GOD

When your fear cometh as desolation,
and your destruction cometh as a whirlwind;
when distress and anguish cometh upon you.
Then shall they call upon me, but I will not answer;
they shall seek me early, but they shall not find me.
PROVERBS 1:27–28

A little boy waited patiently, day after day, to be allowed to play baseball with the bigger boys on the block. Every game was the same. He sat waiting and never got to play. One day he didn't bother to show up. He found another team on another block where he was needed. His old team came to find themselves short of the number needed to play, so they called on the little boy. The boy said, "If you wanted me so badly, you should have given me a chance to play before. Now it's too late."

Often we treat God the same way. When things are going well, we ignore Him; but the minute things go wrong we run to Him, hoping that He will make everything all right. God is not someone that we should turn to only in times of trial. He should be a part of our whole life, both in good times and bad. We must be sure to include God in everything we do.

PRAYER: Dear God, forgive those times when I seem to forget You. Help me to include You in all I do, think, and feel. Be with me to guide me, now and forever. Amen.

TIME WITH GOD

My son, if thou wilt receive my words,
and hide my commandments with thee;
So that thou incline thine ear unto wisdom,
and apply thine heart to understanding;
Yea, if thou criest after knowledge,
and liftest up thy voice for understanding;
If thou seekest her as silver,
and searchest for her as for hid treasures;
Then shalt thou understand the fear of the LORD,
and find the knowledge of God.

PROVERBS 2:1–5

Following Christ requires our all. In order for us to walk in His footsteps, we must be totally dedicated in body, mind, and soul. We need to listen carefully to the Word of God, and we must learn to apply it. We should spend time in contemplation, using our minds to gain a deeper understanding of God's will. We should open our hearts in order to feel God's presence in our lives. We should praise God with our voices, and shout His glories. We should talk with other believers, and share our questions and experiences.

We devote such great energies to the acquisition of material goods. Wealth is so appealing. Yet we fail to understand that true wealth comes only through a relationship with God. The knowledge of God is worth more than the finest riches. God desires that we pursue Him with the same devotion that we pursue material gain. Let that be our aim.

PRAYER: Lord God, no matter what I own, what I might possess, without You I have nothing. Turn my sight from this world, dear God, and help me to seek only You, body, mind, and soul. Amen.

FAITH TO RESIST

He layeth up sound wisdom for the righteous:
he is a buckler to them that walk uprightly.
PROVERBS 2:7

A teenage girl found herself continually tempted by her friends to do things she knew she shouldn't. Once she was offered drugs, occasionally she was offered alcohol. Often she was approached by boys who tried to take advantage of her. Her constant reply was that she was a Christian. Usually she was made fun of for her faith. One time, however, a friend asked her why her faith made such a difference. The girl replied, "I really want to do what God tells me to do. When I do what He wants, I feel better about myself. When I do wrong, I feel terrible. I'd rather feel good inside and have people make fun of me than feel lousy and give in to temptation."

Faith like that is hard to have. It is easy to give in to temptation when it constantly attacks you. But it's good to know that when we resist the temptations God makes it all worthwhile. He makes us feel good about ourselves and gives us even more power to resist in the future.

PRAYER: Dear Father, I am faced by so many temptations. Help me to resist them. Grant that I might rely on Your will and power. Be with me in every situation. Amen.

GOOD PATHS

Then shalt thou understand righteousness,
and judgment, and equity;
yea, every good path.
PROVERBS 2:9

Jesus Christ selected for Himself a band of twelve rough, rugged men to be His disciples. These men knew very little of qualities like gentleness, compassion, kindness, and giving. Prior to Jesus' coming to them, they had very little reason to consider any of these traits. Their paths were many, but none would have been considered good. None, until Christ came along.

During their three years with Jesus, the disciples learned everything there was to know of these qualities. They came to understand all that Jesus tried to show them. They carried these qualities of goodness into the world and taught others to follow them.

If we will take time to spend with Christ in prayer, Bible reading, and devotion, we, too, will learn these traits. We will learn to follow the good paths that Jesus followed. This is what it means to be a Christian. The key is in spending time with God in order to learn them.

PRAYER: Remind me, heavenly Father, that I should spend time with You today and every day. Make me a disciple of Yours, eager to learn all that You would teach me. Amen.

DON'T BLAME GOD

To deliver thee from the way of the evil man,
from the man that speaketh froward things;
Who leave the paths of uprightness,
to walk in the ways of darkness;
Who rejoice to do evil,
and delight in the frowardness of the wicked.
PROVERBS 2:12–14

I recently visited a woman in the hospital. She didn't seem too happy to see me, and after awhile, she let me know why. "God is doing this to me," she said. "He is punishing me because I'm not a church woman. He just waits for someone to make a mistake, then He gets them."

Isn't it strange that people think of God this way? God doesn't want anyone to suffer. He never punishes people arbitrarily. Nor does He turn His sight from those who do wrong. God will finally be the judge of all people, and true justice will be served, but to think that God acts unfairly and without cause is absurd. God loves all human beings and wants the best for them. His love knows no bounds, and when we suffer or struggle, He struggles with us. God is with us in both good times and bad, but He is never to be blamed for our misfortunes. Instead, He is to be praised and thanked for all the wonderful blessings we receive each and every day. There is no place that we can go where God will not be with us. This is the real meaning of blessed assurance. God is with us. Hallelujah!

PRAYER: Oh, thank You, dear Lord, that I am never out of Your sight. You are with me always. Grant that I might feel Your presence each and every day. It is good to know I am never alone. Amen.

PRODIGAL CHILDREN

For her house inclineth unto death,
and her paths unto the dead.
None that go unto her return again,
neither take they hold of the paths of life.
PROVERBS 2:18–19

A young man left for college and found that, once on his own, it was easy to sleep in on Sunday morning. As the weeks passed, church became a memory, and the young man found himself attracted to different activities, not many of them healthy. By the end of his first year, the young man had no connection left with the church. His grades were terrible; his health was ruined; his friends had all turned from him; and he found himself helpless and hopeless. The young man took his life and wrote in his parting note, "I have nowhere to turn. No one wants me around. I've even slammed the door on God."

How sad that the young man didn't understand God better. This young man is no different than the prodigal son in Luke's gospel story. God waits for us continually, standing ready with open arms to receive us to Him. It is important that we know that we can always go back to God. All other paths lead to destruction and pain. How wonderful it is to know that the road to God is never blocked. We cannot do anything to make God stop loving us.

PRAYER: Thank You, Father, for extending Your loving arms to me. If I should stray from Your path, guide me back into Your sight and care. I never want to be without You in my life. Amen.

GOD'S TREASURES

For the upright shall dwell in the land,
and the perfect shall remain in it.
PROVERBS 2:21

My grandmother had a special cedar box in which she kept all of her prized possessions. I used to sit with her at the kitchen table as she would unwrap her treasures. There were old pictures, coins, gems, a lock of hair, a ribbon from a long-past contest, a pair of old glasses, a hand-carved spinning top, and a dozen other knick-knacks. My grandmother would tell the story of each and every one, and the love and affection she shared with those memories will stay with me all of my life.

I think God is a little like that. We are His treasures, and He has set aside a special place for us. Each of us brings forth a feeling of love and affection from God, and He cherishes each one of us. We are each one precious in the good Lord's sight, and He knows our individual stories by heart. It is good to know that God loves us so much that He will keep us for all time in a special place that He has made especially for us. The future glory that awaits all Christians is beyond our wildest imagination, yet we can rest assured that it will far outshine anything we have yet experienced.

PRAYER: Thank You, Lord, that I am one of Your prized posses-sions. Keep me ever in Your care, and cover me with Your divine love and affection. I praise You for Your love, and I will try to be a fond remembrance in Your heart. Amen.

OBEDIENCE

My son, forget not my law;
but let thine heart keep my commandments:
For length of days, and long life, and peace,
shall they add to thee.

PROVERBS 3:1–2

It is easy to see the Bible as a book of "don'ts" rather than a book of "do's." The "Thou shalt nots" far exceed the "Thou shalts." This is not a way for God to control us, for there is nothing farther from His intention than that. But it is merely a show of His great love for us that He offers these instructions to us in order to make our lives better. Our God is a God of order and sense. He knows infinitely more than we can ever hope to, and He shares His knowledge with us to help us through our lives.

If we can learn to be obedient to the will of God, we will find that life becomes a little easier to live, and a lot more fulfilling. Life ceases to be such a struggle, and it becomes a joy. God sent Christ to fight the battle for us. He has become the victor, our victor. To His disciples Jesus said, "Peace I leave with you, my peace I give unto you" (John 14:27). He says the same to us. If we can learn to be more obedient to God, this peace and assurance will be ours throughout our entire lives.

PRAYER: Dear God, help me that I might learn to rest in Your peace. Life can be so difficult, and I know I cannot handle everything on my own. Be with me, guiding me, and helping me to follow Your commandments always. Amen.

LOGIC AND REALITY

Trust in the LORD with all thine heart;
and lean not unto thine own understanding.
PROVERBS 3:5

The resurrection of Jesus Christ caused so much difficulty for His disciples. They had finally gotten themselves used to the fact that Christ was gone, then quite suddenly He reappeared. Logical, rational thinking told the disciples what they knew to be reality: Christ was dead, and nothing could change that. God, however, defies logic and often transcends what we perceive to be reality.

The reality of the resurrected Christ was there for all to see. It was not until the disciples accepted as a fact what they could not fully understand that they were transformed into the foundation builders of the Christian Church.

That same resurrected Christ can transform us today. If we will just learn to accept a God Who is greater and more powerful than the limits of our minds can grasp, we will begin to experience God more fully. Faith is not without reason, but it is always beyond reason.

PRAYER: Help me, Father, to accept what I do not understand, to believe that which I cannot see, and to trust that which is beyond my comprehension. Amen.

My Identity

Be not wise in thine own eyes:
fear the LORD, and depart from evil.
It shall be health to thy navel,
and marrow to thy bones.
PROVERBS 3:7–8

A law student looked for honors and approval from his professors and his peers. His motivation was to "look good" in all that he did. He pursued unbelievably high standards, and when he eventually failed, he was crushed. All of his work to come out on top provided him with nothing. He left law school feeling cheated, and like a failure.

It is easy to fall into a trap of trying to live up to society's standards. We try to look good for other people. We play at popularity games and try to impress others with our position and prestige. This is sad, because who we should really be trying to please is God. He has created each of us with special gifts and talents, and it is His will that we do nothing more than live up to the potential He created for us. We don't have to try with God to be something we're not. He knows us better than we know ourselves. What is really important for us to do is find out who we really are and try to remain true to that identity. God loves us just as we are, and as long as we believe that God knows what He is doing, we can be satisfied with ourselves as He created us.

PRAYER: Lord, help me to realize my potential. Make me less a person-pleaser and more a God-pleaser. Grant that I might discover my gifts and talents, then assist me to use them as You would have them used. Amen.

CRITICISM AND CORRECTION

My son, despise not the chastening of the LORD;
neither be weary of his correction:
For whom the LORD loveth he correcteth;
even as a father the son in whom he delighteth.
PROVERBS 3:11–12

A college youth moved to a new town and began attending a large eastern university. The boy had been an outstanding high school basketball star, so he anxiously awaited tryouts for the college team. On the first day of tryouts, the young man was astounded at how tough and mean the coach was. The young man made the team and experienced the most strenuous training of his career. Hour after hour he was drilled by the coach, and whenever he made an error, the coach was right there to make him correct it. The team played exceptionally well and went to the NCAA championships. Though the young man didn't care much for the way the coach treated the players, he had to admit that the coach got great results.

It is rarely easy to accept criticism and correction, yet it is important that we heed the word of those wiser than ourselves in order to grow and improve. Often the words we heed may seem harsh or unfair, but if they are offered out of love and concern, they may turn into the sweetest sounds we ever hear.

PRAYER: Lord, let me hear the instructions You know I should hear. Tell me what I must do to grow, and give me the acceptance to deal with those things I would rather avoid. Spare not the rod, but do what You know is best for me. Amen.

Moral Values

She is more precious than rubies:
and all the things thou canst desire
are not to be compared unto her.
PROVERBS 3:15

A young woman worked for years to get a management position with a large corporation. She put out excellent effort, and finally it paid off. She began to travel, and new opportunities opened up for her. Everything seemed to be going the way she always dreamed it might. Her success appeared to be complete.

Then she found out that the corporation was involved in some illegal activities. As time passed, she realized that the business was deeply involved in terrible acts of cruelty and unethical practices. The young woman was a long-time Christian, and she was doubly sensitive to the wrongful acts. Faced with such revelations of the corporation's illegal dealings, she found herself with no alternative but to quit.

It is refreshing to know that some people still take their moral values seriously enough to let them rule their lives. It would have been simple for the woman to look the other way and pretend she didn't know what was happening. Instead, she let her heart, governed by the truth of Christ, be her guide. A right relationship with God will always be worth more than personal gain. No greater treasure can be found.

PRAYER: Lord, I so often pursue selfish goals. Help me to remember that nothing in life has value if I do not have a good relationship with You. Be with me, I pray. Amen.

THE TREE OF LIFE

She is a tree of life to them that lay hold upon her:
and happy is every one that retaineth her.
\text{PROVERBS 3:18}

In the Garden of Eden stood two trees: the tree of the knowledge of good and evil and the tree of life. There were other trees, but these were the two most important. God forbade Adam and Eve to eat from the tree of knowledge, but they disobeyed and ate from it anyway. The story goes that Adam and Eve were exiled from the garden due to their disobedience. Was it for punishment that God made Adam and Eve leave the garden, or was it mercy?

God doesn't want any of us to suffer, especially eternally. His action with Adam and Eve made it impossible for them to eat from the tree of eternal life, thus ensuring that they could not live forever in their fallen state. In His infinite love, God provided us with another way. He gave us a new tree of life, His Son, Jesus Christ.

Christ died to undo the harm done by Adam and Eve's disobedience. Once He reconciled us to God, God invited us to once more share in the fruit of the tree of life. Through Christ, we have the promise of eternity in God's heavenly home. It is with this promise that we truly attain wisdom.

PRAYER: Thank You, O Lord, for giving me the chance to have eternal life. Through Your love in the life, death, and resurrection of Your Son, Jesus Christ, I have come to know Your glory. Amen.

LEARNING TO TRUST

My son, let not them depart from thine eyes:
keep sound wisdom and discretion:
So shall they be life unto thy soul,
and grace to thy neck.
Then shalt thou walk in thy way safely,
and thy foot shall not stumble.
PROVERBS 3:21–23

A businesswoman impressed everyone she met with her poise and confidence. Whenever there was an important decision to be made, she didn't even hesitate. Her coworkers came to her for her advice and counsel. She built a reputation for her calm manner and smooth, level head. She instilled trust in everyone she met.

Once she was asked why she was so sure of herself. Her reply? "I grew up being taught to trust. I trust that God is always with me, and knowing that, I can trust that He will help me make good choices. Even though I might make mistakes, I trust that God will always bring good from them."

This is the kind of faith God wants us all to have. Life is less of a burden when we realize that God will be there to bring good from every situation. God is unchanging. His good works continue today and forever. Trust in the knowledge that God will never leave. He is with us in all things.

PRAYER: Help me to believe, to trust, to know. Cast away my doubts, and reassure me that no matter what might happen, You will always be with me. Stand beside me as I grow in faith, and grant me Your peace. Amen.

GOD SEES IT ALL

Be not afraid of sudden fear,
neither of the desolation of the wicked, when it cometh.
For the LORD shall be thy confidence,
and shall keep thy foot from being taken.
PROVERBS 3:25–26

A teacher returned to her classroom to find that chaos had broken out. Paper, pencils, and erasers were flying through the air; pictures were drawn on the blackboards and walls; children were running all around the room; and the noise was deafening. One little girl sat quietly in the back corner, refusing to enter into the mischief. As the teacher began to scold the class, she remembered the little girl who was well behaved. After class, she pulled the young child aside and told her how much it meant to her that she had remained silent and obedient.

Often we feel as though our good acts are missed. When we don't receive credit and acclaim, we feel cheated. What we need to remember is that none of our actions go unnoticed by God. He sees our every move, and He applauds us when we refuse to do those things that we know we should not but that our society seems to approve of. Our reward will never come from this life but from the life that awaits us with our heavenly Father. His blessing is ever with us if we will only be patient and believe.

PRAYER: Father, often I feel as though my good behavior is ignored or forgotten. Forgive me for being prideful, and help me to know that You see me at both my best and worst, and love me all the time. Amen.

Love Your Neighbor

Devise not evil against thy neighbour,
seeing he dwelleth securely by thee.
PROVERBS 3:29

Who is my neighbor? It is a question that we ask ourselves all the time. Christ calls us to love our neighbor as we love ourselves. Though this sounds easy, it doesn't take long to discover that it is not. Not all of our neighbors are lovable people. Is a man who commits murder our neighbor? Is the man who deals drugs or the youth who takes them? Are the people who persecute us our neighbors? Christ's answer to all of these questions would be "Yes!"

If another person does wrong, then God will ultimately judge that person accordingly. We do not have that right. God is interested in our ability to become like Him. Christ gave us a model to follow, and He loved some of the most unlovable characters of His day. We need to do likewise. If we rely on our own powers to love the unlovable, we will fail miserably; but with the love of Christ centered deeply in our hearts, we will be able to love even our enemies.

PRAYER: God, help me to learn love for all people. Let me give of myself and sacrifice my own pride in order to serve other people. Your love is the greatest force on earth. With Your help I can come to know unconditional love, and I can come to be able to give it away. Fill me, Father, with a caring that will never end. I pray this in Christ's most holy name. Amen.

NO GAIN IN ENVY

Envy thou not the oppressor,
and choose none of his ways.
PROVERBS 3:31

A young Mexican immigrant worked on a midwestern tomato plantation for meager wages. His foreman was a hard man who drove his workers to the point of exhaustion. The young man worked diligently, saving every cent he made, vowing that he would become successful and powerful. Daily he saw the foreman sit in the shade with a cool drink, and the immigrant dreamed of a day when he, too, could bask in the shade while others labored in the hot sun. After many years his dream came true. He rose in favor with the plantation owners, and he was put in charge of some of the fields. He tried to be hard and stern and to lounge in the shade drinking cool drinks, but he found he was unhappy. No one liked or respected him, and he felt guilty because he knew how hard the laborers worked. He attained his dream but found nothing in it but emptiness.

There is nothing to be gained by envying those who are in places of authority over us. We may find that we are mistreated, but it is far better to endure minor suffering than to do that which is displeasing to God. God doesn't want us to choose the ways of the oppressor but in all things to choose Him.

PRAYER: Father, please help me to walk in the way of the humble and meek. Keep me from straying into pride and envy. Help me to see the blessings I have been given, rather than long for the things I must do without. Amen.

SPREADING GOD'S LOVE

The curse of the LORD is in the house of the wicked:
but he blesseth the habitation of the just.
PROVERBS 3:33

I have had the pleasure of knowing one of the most faithful families around. The entire family is an inspiration. The mother and father are two of the most loving, caring, devoted people I know, and their two teenage daughters possess a powerful faith and charming personalities. Their home is a haven of peace and comfort. They are always entertaining company because all who enter their home feel the special warmth and joy.

The family is quick to acknowledge that their love and unity come from one source and one source only. They are bound together through the love of Christ. In homes where Christ is king and ruler, it is easy to feel God's blessing. There is no conflict or problem that can upset the blessing that God puts upon a faithful household. There is a special peace which God offers to those people who draw upon His love in order to share it with others. Before we can hope to spread the love of God in our own private worlds, we must first learn to spread it in our own homes, with our own families. It is often harder to keep peace and care with those closest to us, but with God's help, it can be the most blessed peace of all.

PRAYER: Come, O Lord, to be the head of my household and the unifier in my family. Let my home be a haven of comfort and joy. Let my love for those closest to me be the special love that You alone can give. Amen.

APPRECIATING INSTRUCTION

Hear, ye children, the instruction of a father,
and attend to know understanding.
PROVERBS 4:1

Young people are so eager to begin making their own decisions. When it comes to staying out late, how to dress, what to eat, with whom to associate, teenagers want their independence. Learning to make these choices is a part of growing up and maturing, but it takes time to learn to make wise choices. It also takes help. Though young people often resist the guidance and advice of their parents, there is much to be learned from adults who have lived through many of the situations teenagers will face.

We are often just like children when it comes to the instruction of our heavenly Father. There is no situation that He does not know all about, yet we often resist His instruction or ignore His guidance. It is the wise person who learns to take sound advice. As we grow in our faith in God, we also grow in our ability to accept His instruction. It is only as we grow older that we begin to appreciate the decisions our parents made in our behalf as we were growing up. It is also true that when we mature spiritually, we fully appreciate the rules that God has made for us.

PRAYER: Dear God, at times I act like a child in my faith. Help me to receive Your instruction with an open heart and mind. Grant me the wisdom to know that You are always trying to help me grow and to keep me on the path that I should follow. Amen.

WISDOM OF THE HEART

Forsake her not, and she shall preserve thee:
love her, and she shall keep thee.
PROVERBS 4:6

An older friend of mine always lived by the rule "Let your conscience be your guide." Whenever he was faced with a tough decision, he said, "I stop thinking, and I start feeling." For this wise old gentleman, wisdom came from listening not so much to his mind, but more to his heart. He always told me that he knew deep inside whether or not he was making a good choice. Whenever he tried to do what he knew wasn't right, a feeling crept over him, and he could not rest until he did what was right.

Truly, God has given each of us a conscience, a "still small voice," an inner wisdom which guides us and comforts us when we remain true to its instruction. When we choose to ignore the wisdom of our consciences, we face feelings of guilt and anxiety. When we pay close attention to the wisdom of our hearts, we find that there is special comfort. Doing what we know to be right offers not only freedom from guilt but also a joy which comes forth from our souls. Christ rejoices each time we open ourselves to the guidance of the Holy Spirit in our lives. Often God speaks to us through our consciences. If we will listen, God will preserve and keep us.

PRAYER: O heavenly Father, I reach out to Your guidance and will. Fill me with a special wisdom so that I might always choose to follow the right path. Shine Your light before me so that I will never stray. Amen.

GOOD INSTRUCTION

Hear, O my son, and receive my sayings;
and the years of thy life shall be many.
I have taught thee in the way of wisdom;
I have led thee in right paths.

PROVERBS 4:10–11

Many times I have heard parents lament, "What have I done wrong?" Parents are all too willing to take the blame when their children make poor choices or get themselves into trouble. Parents want so much for their children to succeed and have pleasant, carefree lives. That is why there is special joy in seeing children succeed. Mothers and fathers can feel pride and take some credit for their children when those children do well. It is an honor to the parents of children who succeed, that the parents have done a good job. When parents take interest in their children and treat them with respect and care, they are giving them as great a gift as is possible.

Our heavenly Father has tried to instruct us in the ways that lead to eternal life. He has allowed us to make our own choices, though, and we must take responsibility for them, bad or good. It is His greatest wish that we follow the wisdom of His will. When we do so, it is to His glory as well as ours that we have learned well. By listening to our heavenly Father, our lives are enriched, and the years of our lives will be multiplied.

PRAYER: O God, You have been such a loving Father. Forgive me that I have often ignored the instructions You have given me for my sake. Help me to follow Your will and remain steadfast in my commitment to You. Amen.

Avoiding Sin

Enter not into the path of the wicked,
and go not in the way of evil men.
Avoid it, pass not by it, turn from it,
and pass away.
PROVERBS 4:14–15

There are plants in nature which are lovely to look at, but they are deadly. There are animals which seem harmless and even attractive that are dangerous. In life, there are many things which seem appealing, yet they have hidden traps. Sin is a lot like that. Most sins are attractive and tempting. We find ourselves desiring things which could possibly harm us. Often we are lured by things which we know will hurt us, but we want them badly enough to take that risk.

It doesn't make sense that we would do things which we know will harm us. The wages of sin is death, and yet it seems that we pursue sin believing that its wages are the finest reward we could possibly attain. A wise person avoids life threatening situations at any cost. That is what we should do as Christians. We should do everything in our power to avoid sin, which should be as odious to us as death itself. It is not enough to try not to sin; we should do anything in our power to avoid it, turn from it, move as far away from it as possible, and leave it as far behind as can be. It is by a conscious effort that we avoid sin, just as it is by choice that we do good.

PRAYER: May I choose the right path, almighty God, turning from what I know You would not have me do, in order to pursue what is fitting in Your sight. Guide me through the power of Your Holy Spirit. Amen.

GUIDING LIGHTS

But the path of the just is as the shining light,
that shineth more and more unto the perfect day.
PROVERBS 4:18

A young woman worked at a factory which was about ten blocks from where she lived. She could walk to work, but to do so, she had to cross a railroad bridge which was treacherous going when the sun began to set. During the winter months, it was doubly dangerous due to slippery conditions, as well as darkness. The woman would have avoided the crossing altogether had it not been for the crossing guard. Each evening, as the woman approached the crossing, the guard waved a lantern to signal that he awaited. Using the powerful light, he would lead the woman by the hand across the bridge. Throughout her life, the woman never forgot the kindness and help of the older crossing guard.

The lives of those people who are touched by the love of Christ are like guiding lights to others who have yet to find Christ in their lives. They can provide guidance and help, and they shine forth as bright examples of how good life can be. God's light can shine through us if we will only let it. We have the opportunity to show others the difference that Christ can make. When we live life empowered by the light of God, we live as He wishes we would.

PRAYER: Father, please make me a light for my world. Let me shine forth with Your goodness, care, and love. Let all who look to me see Your grace. Help me to magnify the saving light of Christ which You have lovingly given me. Amen.

WHERE'S YOUR HEART?

Keep thy heart with all diligence;
for out of it are the issues of life.
PROVERBS 4:23

Jesus said, "Where your treasure is, there will your heart be also" (Matthew 6:21). What we feel and believe are the truly precious and meaningful things in our lives. If we don't commit ourselves to what is good and right, then we are empty. Moral poverty occurs when we place things above relationships. Christ sent His disciples out into the world without possessions, but no one in history has known more wealth than those chosen men who walked with Jesus. It is when we choose to walk with Jesus that we can find out what true riches are.

In today's world, it is easy to get distracted by so many things. Lifestyles that seem so appealing are presented in magazines and on television. The "good life" requires money, good looks, nice clothes, the right car, the right house, and the right mate. At least that's what we're supposed to believe. But it is only when we can free ourselves from the pursuit of such things that we can begin to enjoy life the way God intended it. Money cannot buy happiness, nor can it bring us life. Christ brings us life, and He brings it most abundantly. He is the real treasure, and as long as our hearts remain with Him, our lives will truly be rich.

PRAYER: Dear Father, forgive me when I lose sight of what is really important in life. Help me to keep my eyes focused on Your truth. Enable me to show others that You are the real treasure in life. Amen.

LOOK FORWARD

Let thine eyes look right on,
and let thine eyelids look straight before thee.
PROVERBS 4:25

When I was in high school, I was quite a runner. Day after day I would train, running seventeen miles in the morning and seventeen miles at night. I ate all of the proper foods, took good care of myself, got plenty of rest, and I followed the instructions of my coaches. One of the most important instructions they ever gave me was: When you're in the race, keep your head straight and look forward. Never turn your head. If you do, you'll break your stride, and it could cost you the race. I saw it happen time and time again. Runners would cast just a quick glance over their shoulders to see where the other runners were, and that was all it took. They would stumble, lose concentration, and the other runners would catch up and pass.

The rule is one that we, as Christians, should learn to follow. As long as we keep our eyes on Jesus, we will do fine. It is when we are distracted, when we lose sight of God in our lives, that we get ourselves into trouble. The rule is a simple one, but an important one: "Let thine eyes look right on" (Proverbs 4:25)—right on Jesus Christ our Lord.

PRAYER: Keep my sight straight, almighty God. Let me see only You in my life. Make me aware of Your presence every day, and never let me turn my eyes from You. Be the vision of my life. Amen.

PATHS TO BLESSINGS

Turn not to the right hand nor to the left:
remove thy foot from evil.
PROVERBS 4:27

When recently traveling to my sister's house, I found myself hopelessly lost. She had given me good directions, telling me to stay on a highway until I came to a certain traffic light. I drove down the highway for what seemed like hours. As the miles passed, I began to doubt whether or not my sister had given me the right directions. The doubts grew and grew, until finally I decided to turn off. I headed in the general direction I thought my sister would be, and that was how I got myself lost. As it turned out, I was only a few minutes from the proper light, but because of my doubts, I was led to make a bad decision.

Many times in our lives we will find ourselves in situations where we grow impatient or doubtful. It is during those times that it is most important to hold fast to the promises of God. God is always there, and He knows what is best for us in every situation. It is vital that we not turn to the right or left but stay steadfastly on the path that leads to God. If we will learn to do that, then the blessings of God will be ours in all circumstances.

PRAYER: Almighty God, forgive me when I doubt Your will and guidance. Help me to always have the faith I need to trust and obey. Make me constant in my belief in You. Amen.

STAY WITH GOD

Her feet go down to death;
her steps take hold on hell.
Lest thou shouldest ponder the path of life,
her ways are moveable,
that thou canst not know them.
PROVERBS 5:5–6

A young woman found the stresses and strains of day-to-day life to be too much for her. She sought out a psychiatrist who saw her three times a week. During her therapy, the doctor began to talk to her about her connection with the church. The doctor told her that church was a crutch and that only weak people needed to go there. The young woman was instructed to stay away from the church and give up her dependence on empty religion. The woman took her doctor's advice and quit the church. In the months that followed, the young woman's problems increased until she left even her psychiatrist in deep despair.

The world, which is the stomping ground of the devil, is quick to turn us away from God, offering a hundred other false gods in His place. When we lose God, we've lost everything. We need to beware of people who try to turn our faith from God to other things. Only God can give us the help and support we need to deal with the regular pressures of life. There is no other way, for it is only with God that all things are possible.

PRAYER: There is no answer apart from You, almighty God. In every situation, both good and bad, You are the strength and the hope. You are every good thing. Be with me in everything I do. Amen.

"No Trespassing"

Hear me now therefore, O ye children,
and depart not from the words of my mouth. . . .
Lest strangers be filled with thy wealth;
and thy labours be in the house of a stranger.
PROVERBS 5:7, 10

The sign nailed to the tree said "No Trespassing." The red letters stood out for yards in every direction. But that didn't stop the young boys from climbing the fence in order to reach the apples that grew on the trees on the other side. One day a small boy slipped while he was climbing the apple tree, and he fell onto a pile of sharp branches, cutting himself badly and breaking his ankle. Alone and afraid, the young boy lay crying for hours amidst the tumble of sticks. Finally, the owner of the property happened by. He came out and lifted the boy from the branches. The child was afraid of the wrath of the farmer who had posted such ominous signs, but the old gentleman merely smiled at the boy and said, "I didn't put the signs up to be mean. I put them there to try to keep things like this from happening. It was kindness which caused me to want to protect little boys just like you."

Our loving, heavenly Father gives us rules for the same reason. He is hoping to save us from pain and suffering. When we ignore His guidance, we find ourselves in terrible situations. We can feel confident that God is trying to protect us by His rules. He protects us from strangers who would prey on us and strangers who might mistreat us.

PRAYER: Dear Father, help me to accept the rules You have given me. Guide me that I might always avoid the snares of strangers and the dangers in life. Amen.

WATERS OF OUR CISTERNS

Drink waters out of thine own cistern,
and running waters out of thine own well.
Let thy fountains be dispersed abroad,
and rivers of waters in the streets.
Let them be only thine own, and not strangers' with thee.
PROVERBS 5:15–17

Two young men had been friends since early childhood. They had shared everything. They had gone through the same experiences, and they understood each other perfectly. They were closer than many brothers. No better friends could be found. When they went off to college, they became roommates. Soon after college began, one of the young men fell in love with a beautiful young coed. The other man became jealous of his friend, and he, too, began to woo the young woman, but behind his friend's back. When his friend finally caught on to what was happening, that friendship came to a bitter and hurtful end.

Fidelity, honesty, loyalty, kindness: All of these are attributes of God that we should desire in our own lives. When we violate these principles, we must pay a price. It is never good to desire that which belongs to someone else. Greed and covetousness result, and they lead to ruin. It is best to always find contentment with "the waters of our own cisterns," those things which are ours, given to us by God. When we learn to be satisfied with what we have, we avoid the pain and suffering attached to taking from others what is rightfully theirs.

PRAYER: I have been given so much that is good in my life, almighty God. Make me to appreciate what I have, and to stop longing for things which are not mine to have. Grant that my spirit might be satisfied this day, O Lord. Amen.

Strange Women

And why wilt thou, my son,
be ravished with a strange woman,
and embrace the bosom of a stranger?
Proverbs 5:20

A young woman sobbed, "I just don't know what to believe anymore! I don't feel God with me like I used to." Her life had gone from bad to worse. She had followed in a long line of bad relationships and bad decisions. She had taken and lost a dozen jobs. She had moved from place to place and was swept up in every new fad to come along. She had joined a group of young people who gathered to meditate and chant together. It was the only place that she felt accepted, but even there she found little comfort as her life crumbled around her. Throughout her childhood she had been a member of a church, and now she felt that she was every bit as devoted with her new group. Still, it wasn't enough.

There is no substitute for the truth and saving power of Jesus Christ. Other groups and sects may appear to be sincere and good, but they are "strange women" who lure us from what is right and good to things we should avoid. The Lord has said clearly, "I am the way, and the truth, and the life. No one comes to the Father, except by me" (John 14:6). Other paths may seem good, but they are false paths which lead nowhere. Stay close to God, avoid "strangers," and all will be well.

PRAYER: There is so much that looks good to me, Father. Protect me from the things which would lead me far from You. Steer me back to You when I stray. Guide my steps by Your loving light, almighty God. Amen.

THE WEB OF SIN

His own iniquities shall take the wicked himself,
and he shall be holden with the cords of his sins.
He shall die without instruction;
and in the greatness of his folly he shall go astray.
PROVERBS 5:22–23

A spider toiled along, crafting an amazing web which stretched forth eighteen inches square. Once finished, the spider spun new webs connecting itself to the corners, until a labyrinth of gossamer filled the corner in which it stood. While the spider busily worked, a larger spider silently crept up alongside. At the right moment, the large spider entered the web, and the creator of it was trapped with no escape.

Sin is like a web. As we become occupied with the things we should not be doing, we become oblivious to the dangers that surround us. We feel that we are in control when, in fact, we are in a very precarious position. There is no good end that can come from a life of sin. We become "holden with its cords," and we cannot get loose. Ultimately, we must answer for our actions before God. If we do not repent of our misdeeds, they become a noose around our neck, and through our folly we find ourselves hopelessly separated from God. It is good that we always pay attention to the ways we live our lives. It is when we grow complacent that we stand in the greatest danger of losing that which is most important. With God's help, we will never be ensnared.

PRAYER: Lord, I turn my attention to so many things that I should not. My sight is distracted by so much folly. Forgive me when I stray, and shine forth Your great light that I might follow its beam back to the source of all life. Amen.

No Strings Attached

Do this now, my son, and deliver thyself,
when thou art come into the hand of thy friend;
go, humble thyself, and make sure thy friend.
Give not sleep to thine eyes, nor slumber to thine eyelids.
Deliver thyself as a roe from the hand of the hunter,
and as a bird from the hand of the fowler.

Proverbs 6:3–5

A young woman moved away from home and settled in an apartment in a large metropolitan area. Her parents came out to visit her, and they took pleasure in buying things for her new apartment. Before they left, they stopped in to see her landlord and paid him three months' rent in advance. This was all done out of love for their daughter, but they wouldn't let their girl hear the end of it. Whenever a disagreement arose, they reminded her of all they had done for her. Finally, in desperation, the young woman sent them a check for the rent and for the items her parents had purchased for her. She included a note saying, "Please don't misunderstand, but I want you to take this back. A gift is no good with strings attached to it."

When we look at the "gifts" the world has to offer, we need to be aware of the strings that are attached. There is always some catch. With the gifts of God, however, there are never strings attached. All God's gifts come from the greatest love the world has ever known.

PRAYER: *See that I give and take freely, Father, never placing anyone in bondage by my actions, nor being cast into bondage myself. Allow me to use the wisdom needed to stay clear of those who would buy my devotion, I pray. Amen.*

WAKE UP!

How long wilt thou sleep, O sluggard?
when wilt thou arise out of thy sleep?
PROVERBS 6:9

I sleep every day till noon!" a young woman proudly ex-
claimed. "I can't remember the last time I saw the sunrise."
What a pity that she was so happy that she missed some of
God's greatest beauty. So many people walk through their
entire lives as if they are asleep. They miss the wonder and
glory of the world around them, and they are not even aware
that they are missing anything at all. The person who sleeps
all the time misses so much. The same is true of the person
who closes his eyes to the beauty of God's world.

God made His creation, and He saw that it was good. He
gave dominion over the earth to men and women to share
with them how good it was. Our lives are creations of God,
and they, too, are good. It is important that we embrace the
goodness of our lives and thank God daily for what we have
been given. It is not good to sleep throughout the bulk of our
lives. We should wake up. Wake up to the creation that God
has given us. It is good, and it is right in front of us to enjoy
and take hold of. It was out of God's love for us that our
world was given, and it should be from love that we return
thanks to Him.

*PRAYER: O Father, what a wonderful world You have made. Let
me look at the world through Your eyes in order that I might see it
in all its freshness and light. I rejoice in Your glory, now and
always, almighty God. Amen.*

PRACTICAL JOKES

A naughty person, a wicked man,
walketh with a froward mouth.
He winketh with his eyes, he speaketh with his feet,
he teacheth with his fingers;
Frowardness is in his heart, he deviseth mischief continually;
he soweth discord.
Therefore shall his calamity come suddenly;
suddenly shall he be broken without remedy.
PROVERBS 6:12–15

A college student loved to play practical jokes. Whenever he found an opportunity, he pulled a gag on one of his friends. No one was safe from his onslaught. Eventually the people he associated with avoided him and hated to be around him. Only when he was alone and lonely did he realize that he had been wrong. He attempted to reconcile with his friends, but they had too often heard his apologies, just to be the butt of another unkind joke. The young man who chose to live by the practical joke had to pay the price.

Our actions affect so greatly how our lives will go. We do things which sometimes seem insignificant to us, but to others they are important. One of our largest responsibilities as Christians is to guard our words and actions carefully, always making sure that what we do to others is what we would want to have done to us. Wickedness can take seemingly harmless forms, but once the seed is planted, no matter how small, it can grow forth into a mighty tree, with roots which reach deep.

PRAYER: Lord, I wish to do no one harm. Would that I could, allow me to spread goodness and light wherever I might go. Save me from the calamity which will befall those who live carelessly or foolishly. Amen.

HAUGHTY ATTITUDES

These six things doth the LORD hate:
yea, seven are an abomination unto him:
A proud look. . . .
PROVERBS 6:16–17

The new girl stepped cautiously into the classroom. She flinched as she looked at the people in the room. They were all dressed in the latest fashions, had nice hairstyles, and carried expensive purses and book bags. She looked down at her faded blue jeans and sneakers. A flush came to her cheeks. When she looked up, she saw that many of the girls and boys were looking at her with condescending sneers. She wished she could sink into the floor. Before she could control it, tears came into her eyes, and she turned away to avoid further embarrassment. Out of nowhere a voice came forth, "Hi, my name's Janet. What's yours?" Carefully, the young girl looked up to see a smiling, friendly face.

An attitude can be as damaging as an unkind word or a forceful blow. We wield great power in the way we treat other people. If we think that we are better than other people, it will show in our manner, our looks, our words, and our actions. God despises the proud and haughty attitudes that people develop. Our duty as Christians is to look at all individuals as equals—brothers and sisters whom we can reach out to. When we look down on others, we do not just withdraw our reach to them, but to Christ as well.

PRAYER: Dear Jesus, help me to see Your spirit in all the people I meet. Be sure that I never turn from another person due to pride or haughtiness. Teach me to love those around me as You would love them. Amen.

A LYING TONGUE

These six things doth the LORD hate:
yea, seven are an abomination unto him:
. . .a lying tongue. . .
PROVERBS 6:16–17

The plan sounded like a good one. The gentleman had sat down with each of the people at the retirement village and explained their policy to them. The cash changed hands; the policies were signed; receipts were given; but that was the last any of them ever heard from the gentleman. He had taken advantage of their situation and made them separate from their hard-earned money. All that could be done was to feel badly that they had been taken in. It was hard to accept that people like that could get away with it. It was a crime.

So often the deceivers seem to get away with so much. They lie, cheat, and steal, and then live it up. It seems that the only ones who get ahead are those who are willing to hurt others to do so. Nothing is farther from the truth. God loves those who will be honest and trustworthy. Lying is abominable in the sight of God, and no one who lives by deception will have any place in His Kingdom. The liar will have to answer to God for what he has done, but those who have lived in the truth will be blessed of God. Men and women who remain true to God's will can rest in the assurance of God's grace.

PRAYER: Dear Lord, I hope that I keep my tongue from hurting anyone through lies or deceptions. Purify my thoughts and my words that they may reflect Your grace and love. Amen.

VIOLENCE OR PEACE

These six things doth the LORD hate:
yea, seven are an abomination unto him:
. . .hands that shed innocent blood.
PROVERBS 6:16–17

Just one hundred years ago it was common practice in the western part of the United States to settle differences with drawn guns and knives. The law of the land was survival of the fittest. Justice was decided by whoever held the greatest force and talent at the time. Law officers were often men who wanted nothing more than to shoot other men. During those days, many innocent people died at the hands of ruthless gunmen. Men, women, and children lived in terror, never knowing which day might be their last.

In every age, in every place, there are people who live by the rule of violence. Their regard for human life is minimal, and they inflict pain wherever they travel. They are seen as strong, when in fact they are sadly weak. Their power is very temporary, and they will be required to atone for their wrongs one day before God. How much better it is to live a life of peace and love! Peacemakers, the meek, those who mourn— they are blessed in the sight of the Lord. Better to be numbered among the blessed than to fall among the accursed. It may seem that the instigators of violence rule this world, but it is the rule of Christ that is the real power, and it reigns in the hearts of all who believe in Him.

PRAYER: Rule in my heart with peace and love. Let me do only kindness to those around me, never harm. Grant that I might be protected from the people who would do me harm, yet let me always face others with forgiveness. Amen.

VENGEANCE IS GOD'S

These six things doth the LORD hate:
yea, seven are an abomination unto him:
An heart that deviseth wicked imaginations. . . .
PROVERBS 6:16, 18

The young teacher crossed the parking lot at the end of a long school day. The week before had been unbelievably difficult. Grades had come out, and that always spelled more pressure for the teachers, especially when there were some who didn't quite make the grade. When the young teacher got to her car, she felt her heart sink. All four of her tires had been slashed. It happened all the time. Living in an urban area, and teaching young people who often didn't want to be taught was a constant risk. Every time grades came out, someone decided they were going to get even. Nothing ever seemed to change. Nothing was ever done to catch the kids who did it. She turned away, disgusted, and went back to the school to call for a ride.

A lot of people live for revenge. They hold grudges, let them burn inside, then explode forth to do whatever damage they can. "Vengeance is mine saith the Lord. . ." (Romans 12:19). When someone wrongs you, your duty is to forgive, not to punish. If someone has done you an injustice, God will call that person to answer for his or her actions. Nothing good can come from a spirit of hurt and revenge. It is through forgiveness that God can enter our lives and make everything all right.

PRAYER: Heavenly Father, pride often causes me to plot in my heart against those who have wronged me. Create in my heart a spirit of forgiveness, that I may do everything in my power to heal with Your great healing love. Amen.

ENERGY OR DESTRUCTION

These six things doth the LORD hate:
yea, seven are an abomination unto him:
. . .feet that be swift in running to mischief.
PROVERBS 6:16, 18

B oys will be boys," said the mother of two mischievous young children. Her boys were into everything, causing calamity wherever they went. The children would terrorize other boys and girls, but the excuse was always the same. If the pair caused injury or pain, they were rarely scolded; their mother merely laughed it off and chalked it up to youthful exuberance.

There is a difference between the energy of youth and destructive, disruptive behavior. The curiosity of young children is wonderful, but unwatched, it can turn to disaster. A child with a package of matches can wreak havoc. There is nothing to be gained by letting children rule their own lives. They need guidance to protect them from things that might hurt them or others.

The same is true of God in our lives. We so often need guidance and wisdom in order to avoid disaster. What may seem harmless to us may, in fact, be the path to mischief and away from God. It is wise to ask God's help as we weigh in our hearts what is good and fruitful to do and what is bad or destructive. With His help, we may hope to walk in paths of righteousness and avoid calamity.

PRAYER: There are times, O Lord, when I feel myself drawn to do things that I know I should not do. I all too often rush into situations that I should avoid. Please guide my steps and protect me from straying, Father. Amen.

SPEAKING LIES

These six things doth the LORD hate:
yea seven are an abomination unto him:
A false witness that speaketh lies. . . .
PROVERBS 6:16, 19

The little girl threw herself into a fit, thrashing around on the ground, spitting, and ranting. The crowd stood around her in amazement. Wide-eyed, the little girl pointed at a woman in the crowd, and immediately the magistrates took hold of her and whisked her off to prison. Thus go many stories of the Salem witch trials in America. The fabrications of a few over imaginative children took root and grew to monstrous proportions. Men and women lost their lives because of the lies of babes. A lie is the worst form of stealing a person can commit. It robs the victim of credibility and honor. It strikes silently and cruelly, and often it allows no room for defense. When we lie, we display selfishness like no other.

Jesus said that He was the truth. If we want to get close to Christ, we must put lies and deceitfulness from our hearts. Our words must be kind and reflect the concern and care of Jesus Christ Himself. When we are honest, we take hold of the truth of Christ and spread it to others that we meet. When we lie, even a little bit, we deny the power of truth and reject the goodness that being honest brings. It is by living honest, straightforward lives that we move closer to God in all His glory.

PRAYER: I wish that I could be the person You want me to be, almighty God. I find that I am dishonest, both with You and with myself. Empower me with a spirit of truth, that I might always live honestly and openly in Your sight. Amen.

SPREADING GOSSIP

These six things doth the LORD hate:
yea, seven are an abomination unto him:
. . .he that soweth discord among brethren.
PROVERBS 6:16, 19

The neighborhood gossip got on the phone and eagerly spread the latest dirt. A new neighbor had moved into the area, and the woman could hardly wait to tell her friends what she had seen. "I saw the movers unpack two very large liquor cabinets. I'll bet they drink a lot. And you should have seen the drums and electric guitar that they own. I just know they will play late at night and keep us all awake. You know, you really can't trust young couples these days. They think they own the world." By the time the gossip had spread the word, no one wanted to reach out to welcome the young couple. Frustrated, the young pair felt excluded from the life of their community, and they never could figure out why people treated them so coolly. A year later the young couple moved away, and they never looked back.

Wouldn't the world be a wonderful place if people would spend as much time trying to make peace as they do trying to tear apart? A few choice words can turn an entire community away, but likewise, just a few words can pave a smooth road. We must guard against doing anything that might hurt another human being. It is through kindness and compassion that we display the special love that God has given us to share.

PRAYER: May the words of my mouth always sound sweet and loving. I want to spread peace, not discord. Show me the way, O Lord, that I might help people and show them the love that I would want for myself if I were in their shoes. Amen.

GOD SEES THE BLISTERS

Can a man take fire in his bosom,
and his clothes not be burned?
PROVERBS 6:27

The cub scout troop had waited all spring for the big camping trip to come around. The dozen young boys piled out of the van and began to set up their tents while the adults prepared the evening meal. The camp was set, the meal consumed, and the group settled in around the big campfire for stories and roasted marshmallows. One bag wasn't enough for the group, so the scoutmaster went back to his car to fetch a second. Before leaving, though, he admonished the boys to stay away from the fire. One small fellow, however, was roasting one last marshmallow that got too soft and fell into the edge of the flames. Without thinking, the boy reached to pick it up and pulled back his hand, alarmed and in pain. The scoutmaster came running back, saying, "What did I tell you?" The young boy denied that he had disobeyed, but the blisters sprouting on his fingers belied his words.

When we fall into sin, it does not simply stay in our own hearts. Sin has resulting implications, and they can stretch out in many ways. We may try to deny that we are sinners, but God in His wisdom sees all and can uncover the "blisters" that sin leaves on our souls. Our coverings bear the burn marks that rise from the fiery passions that occur in our hearts.

PRAYER: Fire can destroy or purify. Guard me from the fire which consumes, and cover me with the fire which cleanses. Make me pure in the fire of Your love, removing from my life the ash and soot of the fires of sin. Amen.

STEALING FROM GOD

Men do not despise a thief,
if he steal to satisfy his soul when he is hungry.
PROVERBS 6:30

A man watched an old woman as she made her way through the town market. As she stood in front of the bread rack, she carefully looked around her, then, confident that she was not being watched, she slipped a loaf under the cover of her shawl into a shopping bag. The man rushed to the counter to tell the owner what he had just witnessed. The grocer said to the man, "I know, I know. She's done it for years. She never takes much; only enough to feed herself and her cat. Maybe I shouldn't let her get away with it, but it's the least I can do. She's friendly and kind, and she does nice things for people whenever she can. I would want it done for me if I were in her place. What does it hurt?"

Stealing is never right, but sometimes it makes more sense, and we can understand when the motive isn't greed. Sometimes we act just like the woman in our spiritual lives. We take only what we need, and we don't pay God anything for what we get. There are many times when we find ourselves so starved spiritually that we take and take and take, but give little back. God understands that, and He knows that by feeding us when we hunger, we are being strengthened in a way that will enable us to give to others later on. When we come to a place where we can begin giving what has been given to us, then we are truly pleasing to God.

PRAYER: Forgive me for the times when I take without offering anything in return. Fill me with what I need to give to others who have not been as fortunate as myself. Amen.

Ten Fingers

My son, keep my words,
and lay up my commandments with thee.
Keep my commandments, and live;
and my law as the apple of thine eye.
Bind them upon thy fingers,
write them upon the table of thine heart.
PROVERBS 7:1–3

There was a man who spent all his days sitting by an old firehouse, telling stories to the neighborhood children. The youngsters would flock around the man to hear him tell of bygone days. One striking feature of the old gentleman was that around each of his fingers he had tied a different colored string. The children would ask what the strings were there for, and the old man would say that each one was to remind him of something important. This was the way he remembered things.

For everyone who came to him, he had this to share. "You don't need strings to remember the most important things. God gave us ten fingers and Ten Commandments, and if you keep one commandment on each finger, then you'll never forget any of them."

The commandments of God should be as much a part of us as the fingers that are part of our hands. If we take care to remind ourselves of the laws of God, then they will be forever inscribed on the very "table" of our hearts.

PRAYER: I continue to forget the things I should do. Help me to remember what You would have me do. I cannot hope to be the person You want me to be without Your help. Amen.

WE NEED HELP

[I] beheld among the simple ones,
I discerned among the youths,
a young man void of understanding.
PROVERBS 7:7

A small girl set about preparing a menu for her pretend birthday party. She planned a full meal of cookies, cake, candy, ice cream, and potato chips. To drink, there would be lemonade and soda. Her choices were made from her own affection for the treats, but no thought was given to what might be nutritious or keep her from getting sick. Children many times fail to use good sense when they make their decisions. They need guidance in order to avoid unnecessary pain and suffering. Sometimes children resist the advice of their parents, but they need it nonetheless.

When we compare our wisdom with God's, we find that we are simple and dull in relation. We have neither the experience of God, nor the insight. His knowledge so far exceeds our own that we seem naïve and inept. Luckily, God offers His wisdom and knowledge with no strings attached. He does so out of love for us, and He only wants us to avoid the pitfalls that come our way. Christian maturity comes when we can admit that we need help and accept the aid God so freely offers.

PRAYER: Break my spirit of resistance. Help me to be obedient to Your will, Father, as a loving and faithful child. Amen.

THE GIFT OF SPEECH

Hear; for I will speak of excellent things;
and the opening of my lips shall be right things.
PROVERBS 8:6

There was a woman that everyone dearly loved. She never lacked for company, because so many people flocked to spend time with her. She had the ability to engage anyone, old or young, male or female, black or white, intelligent or simple, in delightful conversation. With a beautiful voice she would tell stories of bygone days and share dreams and wishes with anyone who would listen. She was full of compliments but never empty flattery. In every situation, she knew the perfect thing to say. In trouble, she spoke words that soothed, in times of stress she spoke words of comfort, and in good times she knew the perfect joke or anecdote to share.

The gift of speech is a valuable one. It also carries with it great responsibility. We are commanded to avoid silly or coarse speech, but to always use words to uplift and praise. Our words should reflect the presence of God in our hearts. Only the most excellent and right things should spring forth from our mouths.

PRAYER: Let the words of my mouth always produce what is pleasing in Your sight, O Lord. Let me build up, rather than tear down. May my speech reflect my great love for You. Amen.

Guidance for Growth

All the words of my mouth are in righteousness;
there is nothing froward or perverse in them.
They are all plain to him that understandeth,
and right to them that find knowledge.
Proverbs 8:8–9

The crew of young doctors cowered under the tongue-lashing given to them by the chief of surgeons. Each doctor knew that his mentor was right, but it was difficult to receive such harsh criticism. Each doctor also knew that the only reason the chief surgeon was so tough was to make sure they were the best they could be. The man demanded perfection, and he wasn't going to settle for less. Only doctors who wanted to be the best could stand to take the kind of scrutiny the chief surgeon put them under. No matter what else might happen, each new doctor knew that he would receive truth and guidance from the older man. They trusted him because they knew he was doing everything he knew to do to make them the best they could be.

How willing are we to place ourselves in positions to be criticized? It is hard to invite others to tell us what we do wrong and how we can improve. Yet, if we want to grow, we need to have criticism given to us. The Lord offers us guidance as we try to grow, and we can be sure that it will be given to us with the greatest love, even though it is often hard to acknowledge that we are lacking. Thank goodness that God is so patient with us and that He gives us time to change and grow.

PRAYER: Help me to trust the wise counsel of others. I know that I have so much room to grow. Grant that I might have the wisdom to accept the helpful criticism of others, and make me to seek Your ways. Amen.

SHORTCUTS TO RUIN

I wisdom dwell with prudence,
and find out knowledge of witty inventions.
PROVERBS 8:12

A powerful businessman was always looking for ways to cut corners. Any shortcut and cost cutting method he could find, he would use. It didn't matter whether or not the cuts hurt quality or endangered employees. All that mattered was making the most money for the least cost. For a while things worked well, but as time passed, more and more people lost faith in the products that the man's companies produced, and finally he faced financial ruin. All the shortcuts he took seemed to lead to the reward he desired, but in fact, they destroyed the hope of reaching his dream.

There are no shortcuts to wisdom. The knowledge of the heart comes to us from patience, experience, and prayerful reflection. God wishes this wisdom for all of His children, but it comes only over time. Patience is greater than we can begin to comprehend. Shortcuts may look promising in the near future, but it is the person who learns the benefits of waiting who is on the road to true wisdom. It is so pleasing to God when He sees us grow spiritually, and the best way we can show that growth is to learn to say, with Jesus, "Not my will, but thine, be done, O Father, now and forever. Amen."

PRAYER: Keep my feet on the right path, O Lord. Keep me from straying onto roads which seem to be easier to travel but lead nowhere. As long as Your light shines forth before me, I know that all will be well. Amen.

THE SOURCE OF WISDOM

Counsel is mine, and sound wisdom:
I am understanding; I have strength.
By me kings reign, and princes decree justice.
By me princes rule, and nobles,
even all the judges of the earth.
PROVERBS 8:14–16

S olomon was considered to be the wisest of all human beings. His judgment was sound and fair. Subjects traveled
from all over Israel to seek his counsel. His word was law
because people believed that there was no greater mind in all
the world. Whatever Solomon decreed, the people gladly
accepted. Solomon did nothing more than use the gifts God
had given him in the best way possible. Solomon relied heav-
ily on God's guidance and help. He prayed long and hard for
God to inspire him with special wisdom. Solomon listened at
length to the scribes who read to him from the Scriptures. He
was ever questing after a deeper knowledge of God.

Solomon was able to give great wisdom because he was in
touch with the source of wisdom—God. As much as Solomon
was willing to give himself to God, God was willing to give
Himself right back. God showed that He was willing to do
the same for us, by giving Himself in the person of His Son,
Jesus Christ. All we need do is accept His gift and try to the
best of our ability to follow His example. Like Solomon, we
receive strength and understanding from the God Who gives
us all good things.

PRAYER: Lord, I wish that I could be one with Your Spirit, that
I might spread Your will in this world. You offer so much, and I take
so little. Help me to use what You hold forth, that I might reflect the
blessed light of Your Son, Jesus Christ, throughout this world. Amen.

A CHRIST-LIKE LEGACY

I lead in the way of righteousness,
in the midst of the paths of judgment:
That I may cause those that love me to inherit substance;
and I will fill their treasures.

PROVERBS 8:20–21

A poor woman called her children to her soon before her death. She sat them down and told them, "I never had money or nice things, and I'm sorry that I don't have good things to leave you, but I always tried to do what was right by you. If I brought you up right, so that you do what you know is right to do, then I have left you more than any amount of money."

The woman was right. The things money can buy are temporal; they wear out, break down, and then they're gone. A good sense of values is worth more than all the money in the world. The greatest gift we can hope to give another human being is that of wise counsel. We often hope that we can leave a legacy, a testament to our lives, after we die. There is no more fitting legacy than helping other people learn to love life and enjoy it every day. We can make our lives an example of the truth of Christ, letting others see just how much Christ can change lives for the better. He will "lead us in the paths of righteousness," but only so that we might have something of substance, something that will last long after our material wealth has gone. That is the real treasure, and God gives it freely to all who will take it.

PRAYER: I try to turn my eyes from material gain, to true gain: the gain of eternal life. Help me to follow Your instructions that I might have Your righteousness. Grant me a small portion of Your holy inheritance. Amen.

THE GRAND CANYON

When he prepared the heavens,
I was there: when he set a compass upon the face of the depth:
When he established the clouds above:
when he strengthened the fountains of the deep.
PROVERBS 8:27–28

The three weeks before the trip seemed to drag on, and the little boy counted the days until his uncle came to pick him up. His uncle was going to take him out of the city to drive across the country to California. It was as exciting as a trip to the moon.

The day for the start of the trip came, and the pair set out on their adventure. When the trip was over, the little boy was asked what had been the best part of the trip. Without hesitation he said, "The Grand Canyon!" When asked why, the boy said, "My uncle said that you could see all the layers of time which have gone by, by looking at the stripes in the rock. He told me that the very first layer was put there by God, and that God was there when every other layer was laid on top. But you know what? He also said that before God ever started making the Grand Canyon, He started thinking of me and loving me!"

We may look on our world with wonder and amazement, but nothing is more amazing than the fact that it was all made for us, out of God's infinite love for us. We owe Him thanks and praise every day for giving so much.

PRAYER: O Lord of majesty and grace, You have indeed created a beautiful world for our comfort and joy. Thank You for sharing this great gift with me. Help me to appreciate it more fully and to care for it with wisdom. Amen.

WATCH THE GATE

Blessed is the man that heareth me,
watching daily at my gates,
waiting at the posts of my doors.
PROVERBS 8:34

A security guard worked at the same job, watching the gate of a chemical plant, for fifteen years. For that entire time, no one had ever tried to break into the plant. The guard watched television, read books and magazines, drank sodas, and walked the grounds. Often he would doze off, passing the long, tedious hours in slumber. It hadn't always been that way. When he was first hired, he had sat alertly at his post, making his rounds promptly and completely. He had spent hours working on ways to improve security at the factory. That hadn't lasted long. The dull routine of the work and the late hours took their toll. As time passed, so did the guard's enthusiasm.

One night, while the guard slept, three men broke into the plant and made off with thousands of dollars' worth of valuable chemicals and drugs. In an instant, the guard lost his position because of his inattention when it mattered most.

Christians need to take heed. Our attention must be on the Lord. We never know what might lie ahead, so we should consciously try to be the best we can be in all circumstances. If we live each day as if it is the day we will meet our Maker, then we won't be embarrassed on the day it finally comes.

PRAYER: I pray that I might be alert and fully awake to my duties as Your loving disciple. As I follow Your will, let me not grow weary or tired, but fill me with every energy that I might be ready when my time comes. Amen.

THE GIFT OF LOVE

Wisdom hath builded her house,
she hath hewn out her seven pillars:
She hath killed her beasts;
she hath mingled her wine;
she hath also furnished her table.
PROVERBS 9:1–2

When I first began my ministry, I did so as a student in seminary. I had never served people officially before, and it surprised me when I was treated with so much respect and consideration. People showed me that they had faith in me, and it helped me to be able to minister to them, many of whom were much older than I was. I was treated royally, and I was a little embarrassed because I didn't think I deserved it.

When we come into God's presence, we may find ourselves surprised at how well God treats us. We come to Him as sinners, ashamed and afraid, and He treats us like kings and queens. We are not strangers who receive the lesser quality, but we are sons and daughters, welcomed home and treated to only the best. God lays out the finest for His children, and it doesn't matter that we are undeserving. Children rarely deserve the love their parents have for them, but love, true love, cannot be earned. Love is a gift, and God freely gives His love to each and every child who will accept it. All we must do is accept the gift, not earn it. Wisdom comes to those who don't question the giver, but accept the gift with gratitude.

PRAYER: Gracious and giving God, I cannot give You great enough thanks for all You offer to me, a humble child. Help me to give others some of the precious, unconditional love that You have given me. Amen.

SCORNERS VS. WISE MEN

He that reproveth a scorner getteth to himself shame:
and he that rebuketh a wicked man getteth himself a blot.
Reprove not a scorner,
lest he hate thee: rebuke a wise man,
and he will love thee.
PROVERBS 9:7–8

A woman was given a project to do for a large advertising agency. She selected two other women to work with her on the project. The supervising woman worked closely with the other two for weeks, and finally a finished product was presented to the clients for approval. The project came back with comments, and a list of changes was called for. The supervisor called in the two other women and shared the list. One of the women sat calmly and listened to the proposal, while the other woman flew into a rage. She felt that she was being insulted, and she criticized the clients for not knowing good work when they saw it. When the supervisor defended the clients' rights, the woman slammed down her portfolio and stormed from the office saying that she quit.

If we can't take criticism, we cannot hope to grow. Growth comes from finding our weaknesses and working to build them into strengths. When we try to help people who aren't willing to admit they can grow, they deal with us in anger. When God calls for us to change, how will we react to His request? Will it be with anger, or will it be with humble obedience?

PRAYER: Often pride gets in the way of my maturing spiritually, O Lord. Help me to receive criticism with grace and to work always to improve myself. Soften my heart to the comments of others, and let me deal with others in love and care. Amen.

REMEMBER THE SCRATCH

The fear of the LORD is the beginning of wisdom:
and the knowledge of the holy is understanding.
For by me thy days shall be multiplied,
and the years of thy life shall be increased.
If thou be wise, thou shalt be wise for thyself:
but if thou scornest, thou alone shalt bear it.

PROVERBS 9:10–12

A young woman took a job tending animals at a zoo. Her third week on the job, she was shown how to feed the lions, tigers, and other big cats. Large portions of meat were stabbed by long spears, and then they were stuck through the bars of the cages to the animals. While in training, a piece of meat slipped from the end and lay half in and half out of the cage. The woman moved up and reached to pick up the meat. The lion inside the cage growled and pounced against the bars, reaching through and badly scratching the young woman. Her trainer rushed over and said, "Don't ever do that. Use the stick. If you had been closer and the cat's reach a little longer, you wouldn't be here now. I hope you remember that scratch the rest of your life."

In so many situations, we feel that we are in control, that nothing can happen to us. We forget how truly fragile we are. We become complacent and lose our fear, our respect for things we should remember. The fear of the Lord is nothing more than knowing Who He is and respecting Him. If we learn that fear, all our days will be long, and our lives will be safe and happy.

PRAYER: O Lord, help me to keep from letting down my guard for even one minute. Open my eyes to my limitations and grant that I might acknowledge my shortcomings. Amen.

HAVING GOD WITH US

Treasures of wickedness profit nothing:
but righteousness delivereth from death.
PROVERBS 10:2

A man climbed to the top of the business world by shrewd investments and fast-talking. One of his favorite ploys was to build low-budget housing and then to rent it at rock-bottom prices. Renters would then improve the property, and the man would raise their rent, forcing them to move; then he would re-rent at a higher rate. Though it brought in lots of money, it also brought him a reputation that lasted throughout his life. Everyone knew that he would stop at nothing to make more money, and it little mattered that he hurt many people to make it. When he died, he was one of the wealthiest men in the country, but he was also the loneliest.

Nothing could be worse than facing death alone, without the love of God in your life. All the things money can buy pale in comparison to the worth of having God with us. Taking advantage of other people in order to gain things for ourselves is wrong. It is an abomination in the sight of the Lord, and it builds walls which cannot be broken down. However, if we learn to live our lives for others, we will find the true treasure that God had in store for us. Righteousness delivers us from the death that destroys the very root of our souls.

PRAYER: Father, thank You for never leaving me alone. I have everything I need as long as I have You. Stay close by me, and teach me how to give Your blessed love to others. Amen.

THE VALUE OF HARD WORK

He becometh poor that dealeth with a slack hand:
but the hand of the diligent maketh rich.
He that gathereth in summer is a wise son:
but he that sleepeth in harvest is a son that causeth shame.
PROVERBS 10:4–5

Two nurses were in the running for a staff position in a large metropolitan hospital. One was a hard-working young woman from the Midwest who had striven her whole life to be the best nurse she could possibly be. She studied long and hard and was at the top in her class. She continued to study and learn new techniques and practices. The other was a young man whose father was the hospital administrator. He did his job, but no more. He figured he was the favorite as far as the new position went, so he sat back and awaited the decision. He was shocked when he learned that the young woman had been selected.

There is nothing to be gained by resting on our laurels. Hard work and integrity are important values to possess. If we can learn to be disciplined in our daily work, then we can improve our spiritual discipline as well. It is pleasing to God when we put forth our best efforts. When we refuse to do our best, then we are failing to utilize the talents and gifts that God has given to us all.

PRAYER: I want to be a faithful and devout servant, O Lord, doing all that is required of me, using my talents in the best possible way. Help me to do what is right, keep me diligent, and turn me away from the temptation to avoid my responsibilities. Amen.

The Wise in Heart

The wise in heart will receive commandments:
but a prating fool shall fall.
PROVERBS 10:8

The story is an old one and one that is happening all too often. A couple prepared to leave a party where they had overindulged. The woman was drunk, and her husband only slightly less so. As they began to put on their coats, a friend offered to drive them home. Insulted, the husband refused to even consider it. The husband and wife stumbled to their car amidst the protests of their friends. Despite the warnings and admonitions, the couple sped off in their car. As it rounded a tight curve, it swung out into the oncoming lane and struck another car. Though the husband and wife were only slightly hurt, the other driver and his son were killed.

Foolish people refuse to recognize wisdom, even when it is right in front of them. It doesn't matter who offers the suggestions. Both friends and foes are ignored. When our egos get in the way of clear thinking, we are on a pathway that leads away from God. God glories in the person who will listen to good advice and do what is right. God doesn't give us instruction in order to ruin our good time. His word is offered only to give everyone the chance to live life to the fullest. It is the wise in heart who receives instruction gladly. The fool stumbles down the road to destruction.

PRAYER: *Unplug my ears, O Lord, and let me hear the wisdom of those who care for me. Destroy my foolish pride, and lead me to paths of good sense and smart choices. Keep me from hurting myself and others. Amen.*

STORYTELLING

He that winketh with the eye causeth sorrow:
but a prating fool shall fall.
PROVERBS 10:10

Her uncle had been a wonderful storyteller. In fact, she had never known when to believe him and when to know he was kidding. She had believed the stories of the Amazon and the war, and even of his days as a pro baseball player. She had thought her uncle could do anything. It had been devastating when she had found out that he was an alcoholic and that he would have to be put in an institution. In the years that passed, she found out that her uncle had never been to the Amazon, had never played pro ball, and had even been turned down by the army. She never really got over her disillusionment, and it made her skeptical of everyone she met. She lost faith in heroes.

Each one of us has had a tall tale to tell at some point in our lives. With tongue in cheek, we have put someone on. There is nothing wrong with pulling someone's leg, so long as it isn't a way of life, and we don't do damage by our untruth. We need to be able to trust others. We need honesty. And other people need to be able to trust us. Honesty is a valuable virtue. We have the power to change lives when we speak the truth. If we tell people fables, we lose credibility and weaken our power to help them.

PRAYER: Help me that I never undermine the faith that others have in me. Let me be honest and open, so that I might have the opportunity to make a difference in their lives. Amen.

NOTHING GAINED BY CHEATING

He is in the way of life that keepeth instruction:
but he that refuseth reproof erreth.
PROVERBS 10:17

The judge watched carefully to see where his golfing partners were. Confident that he wasn't seen, he gave his ball
a hefty kick. The ball traveled forward about twenty-five feet
onto a soft patch of close-cropped grass in direct line with the
green. He saw nothing wrong with it. He had done it as long
as he golfed, and he told himself that his partners did it, too.
On this occasion a booming voice cried out, "Hey, what are
you trying to pull? Your ball was in the trees!" A raucous ver-
bal battle ensued, with both sides accusing the other side of
cheating. Regardless of guilt, the judge always defended himself completely.

We really do kid ourselves when we think cheating is a
way to get ahead. There is nothing to be gained by cheating.
Our victories are empty ones, and we open ourselves to criticism and doubt. We lose our credibility and turn people against
us. It is in honesty and truth that we find fulfillment. God
dwells in truth, and He loves honesty. This is the way of life,
but the way of death is through sin.

PRAYER: I am sorry for the ways that I try to get ahead by dis-
honesty. I am not honest with myself, and then I am not honest
with You. Forgive my deceptions, and lead me in the light of Your
truth, O God, now and forever. Amen.

Spoken from the Heart

The lips of the righteous feed many:
but fools die for want of wisdom.
PROVERBS 10:21

The young woman sat enthralled by the words of the young preacher. She had attended church with her parents when she was young, but she found it boring and stupid. She had managed to avoid church for years, but she began to feel a longing deep inside, and its nagging had led her to this place. The boredom she remembered from her youth was gone. The truth of the preacher's words touched her at the very root of her soul. Tears rolled down her face as she realized all that she had missed over the years. Her heart beat with joy that she at long last felt as though she had come home.

When words of truth are spoken from the heart, they reach out to people to give them a rich blessing. It is important that we request the Spirit's guidance as we speak. When we allow God's words to spring from our mouths, we become agents for His glory here on earth. We have in our power the ability to feed those who find themselves spiritually hungry. May we use that power wisely and well.

PRAYER: Lord, I so want to serve You in all ways. Take my words and make them Yours. Pour out Your grace through my lips, and make my speech a blessing to those who hear. Amen.

After the Storm

As the whirlwind passeth, so is the wicked no more:
but the righteous is an everlasting foundation.
PROVERBS 10:25

The sky turned an ugly black, and the lightning creased the sky. Powerful, rolling thunder echoed for miles, and the bottom of the clouds broke downward into a massive funnel. The tail of the cloud whipped downward until it met the ground. As it touched, debris flew high into the air. The cloud cut through the farmland, clearing the land wherever it wandered. One farm completely disappeared from the face of the earth. Fields were stripped of their growth, and trees snapped sideways like twigs. The fury of the storm mounted, then began to subside. The powerful tail of the tornado whipped once, twice, then shredded, throwing wisps of haze into the air. The tail rose and separated, and then was no more. Nature had claimed victory, reminding everyone where the real power lay.

The future of the evildoer is similar to that which lies in the path of the tornado. In its time it will be swept completely away, and after the coming of the Lord, it will be as if it never existed. But, just like a firm foundation, the true believers will remain standing after the storm. When our foundation is the Lord of all creation, there is nothing that can destroy us.

PRAYER: Be my foundation, Lord. Let the winds sweep past me, but let them never carry me away. My hope and trust is ever in Your love. Amen.

LIVING FAIRLY

A false balance is abomination to the LORD:
but a just weight is his delight.
PROVERBS 11:1

In times long gone, traders would sell grain by the measure of weight to those who would come to them. Many would place stones in the bottom of the bags in order to increase the weight. By the time their ploy was discovered, the sellers were long gone. Many traders made their fortunes by cheating unsuspecting buyers. This practice was widespread, and nothing was done to protect the innocent.

It is a terrible feeling to be cheated and know that we are helpless to fight it. We hate being on the receiving end of other people's selfishness and cruelty. We long for some way to even the score. Thankfully, God has promised that the score will indeed be settled. Those who live by deception will find themselves outside of the grace of God. No one who makes his living by the blood, sweat, and tears of others can be numbered among the children of God. He has turned his back on the ways of the Lord, and so he will pay the penalty. It is comforting to know that God sees all things, and that He will sit in judgment in the last days. Remain steadfast in the Lord, and He will grant you His favor.

PRAYER: O Lord, soften my heart against those who take advantage of me. Guide my dealings that I never take advantage of another one of Your children. Let my life be one of fairness and honesty. Amen.

MUSICAL CHAIRS

Riches profit not in the day of wrath:
but righteousness delivereth from death.
The righteousness of the perfect shall direct his way:
but the wicked shall fall by his own wickedness.
The righteousness of the upright shall deliver them:
but transgressors shall be taken in their own naughtiness.

PROVERBS 11:4–6

A group of children gleefully circled the line of chairs, while music played in the background. When the music abruptly stopped, the children raced to the nearest seat and plopped themselves down. One lone child stood, then walked off the floor, taking a chair with her. The music resumed, and the game continued. Eventually, one boy stood and one boy sat, and the game came to an end.

It is a little too simple to compare life to a game of musical chairs, but in the end of time, there will be winners and there will be losers. Those who pay attention and play by the rules will find that their reward is in heaven. Those who have been inattentive will find that their future will be loneliness and despair.

We live as though we know what tomorrow will bring, when in fact we have no idea. In musical chairs, the participants anticipate the music's end, and they ready themselves to move quickly. In life we should be every bit as ready, so that when the music ceases, we won't be caught napping. Regular prayer and reading of the Scriptures can help us to stay ready.

PRAYER: I'm listening for Your word, O Lord. Guide me by Your love, that I might always be ready to meet You face-to-face. Keep me attentive, Lord, and make sure that I don't slumber.

JUDGMENTS WITHOUT FACTS

He that is void of wisdom despiseth his neighbour:
but a man of understanding holdeth his peace.
PROVERBS 11:12

As a child, I remember a man who lived down the street who frightened me terribly. He was an older man who was paralyzed on his left side. His face was disfigured, and he limped along on a cane. He had a low, gravelly voice with which he used to yell, "You brats stay away from me! Come too close and I'll split your head!" For years I would race past his house, trying not to look at his face. I felt relieved when the old man died, but later found out how lonely and hurt the old man had been. He had lived a hard life, had no friends, and took his frustrations out in the only way he knew how. The man I had once thought was a monster was actually just a poor, lost soul.

I think often of how I misjudged the old man and feel foolish that I never tried to get to know him. I made judgments without knowing all the facts. It truly is the person who is without wisdom who despises his or her neighbor. Those who have understanding refrain from jumping to conclusions, and they hold their peace. There is so much good we can do if we will only be patient and find out all the facts first.

PRAYER: I am too quick to judge, almighty God. Grant me the patience and wisdom I need to live by the rule of gold, that I might treat others as I would like to be treated. Amen.

NEVER ALONE

Where no counsel is, the people fall:
but in the multitude of counsellors there is safety.
PROVERBS 11:14

All the young widow left behind was a note saying, "I could have made it if I just had someone to talk to. I can't stand being all alone. I know my problems aren't so much greater than those of other people, but I need someone to help me solve them. I can't do it by myself anymore."

Out of desperation and loneliness, the woman took her life. This is the tragedy of those who don't know Jesus Christ. With Christ in our hearts we are never alone. God rejoices when we pour out our hearts to Him, confiding our deepest needs and desires. We all need someone to talk to. When there is someone to talk to, we feel happy and fulfilled. The load is taken off our hearts, and we are liberated. God is our savior and protector. He listens to even the smallest of our cries. We can rejoice that we have someone Who understands us so completely and cares for us so totally. When no one else is there for us to talk to, God remains by our side, never leaving, never turning.

PRAYER: My Lord, I need a haven in this stressful world. I need someone who will share my burdens and hear my cries. I need to feel that my cries are being heard. Hear, O Lord, the murmurs from the depths of my heart. Give me peace that passes understanding. Amen.

RETAINING RICHES AND HONOR

A gracious woman retaineth honour:
and strong men retain riches.

PROVERBS 11:16

Judas Iscariot possessed qualities that Jesus considered worthy, or he never would have been selected as a disciple. Judas followed faithfully for the better part of three years as he shared in the ministry of Christ. At a time when he should have been most strong, he proved weak. He gave in to the temptation of the sparkle of silver, and he betrayed his friend and Lord. He had lived so very close to the true treasure: the love of Jesus Christ, and he threw it all away due to his weakness.

Everyone sins. That is sad but true. Often we are weak when we want to be strong. It is vital that we hold on to the love of God in those times when we are most sorely tempted. God offers us His strength when our own strength is not enough. All we need to do is pray for this strength, and it will be given to us. When we fall prey to sin, and we allow it to control us, we join with Judas in betraying the truth of Christ. When we call on God to help us in our weakness, then we have found true wisdom and strength. If we will deal honestly with God, He will shower us with treasure which cannot be taken from us, and honor which testifies to the glory of Christ.

PRAYER: O Lord, I pray that I might make You proud of me. I will try to please You by my actions and praise You with my words. Be with me, Father. Amen.

GOD'S GOODNESS IS STRONG

They that are of a froward heart are abomination to the LORD:
but such as are upright in their way are his delight.
Though hand join in hand,
the wicked shall not be unpunished:
but the seed of the righteous shall be delivered.
PROVERBS 11:20–21

In a small midwestern town a concerned group began a crusade against pornographic materials being sold in public places. Their protest met with resistance, so they hired a firm to investigate the matter for them to see who they were really up against. By the time the investigation was over, it came to light that not only were area businessmen involved, but also the mayor of the town, the chief of police, two school administrators, and three powerful lawyers. The group gave up, as they felt the deck was favorably stacked for the opposition.

Evil is a difficult thing to fight, and it seems impossible to defeat when it is made manifest in a large group of people. It is strange that evil forces seem to have no trouble combining their strength, while often the forces of good never manage to get together. It is comforting to know that in the end, God's goodness is stronger than any amount of evil on this earth. Those who are evil in the sight of the Lord are an abomination, and they will have no part in His heavenly kingdom. The upright are a delight to the Lord, and it is those people who will dwell with God in heaven eternally.

PRAYER: Protect me from those who try to do me harm, O Lord.
In the face of evil, help me to remember that You are God, and evil
has no power over You or those who choose to follow You. Amen.

What We Give

There is that scattereth, and yet increaseth;
and there is that withholdeth more than is meet,
but it tendeth to poverty.
PROVERBS 11:24

During the Great Depression, two families shared a house in Pennsylvania. One family occupied the upper floor, and the other family lived on the lower. The family which lived downstairs was always inviting people in to share what they had. Whenever there was an opportunity for them to help out, they would do so. No matter how much they gave, they always seemed to have enough. The family on the upper floor, however, scoffed at the way the downstairs family lived. They stored all extras in a locker in the pantry. They gave nothing away. It was not until they found that rats had gotten into their pantry that they were sorrowful for what they had done. Interestingly, the rats had not disturbed the downstairs pantry.

Selfishness leads to despair. True joy comes to us not from what we own but from what we are able to give to others. We were put on this earth to serve one another, and when we fail to do so, there is a price to pay. When we give what we have, God will bless us with more, and the blessings will be double because of the joy that giving brings.

PRAYER: Take what I have, Lord, and use it for Your glory. I have nothing except what You have given me. Help me to share from my abundance and to give all that I can to those who are in need. Amen.

The Clown

He that diligently seeketh good procureth favour:
but he that seeketh mischief,
it shall come unto him.
PROVERBS 11:27

There was a man who took it upon himself to dress up like a clown and go into neighboring hospitals to visit sick children. He was not hired to do so, but he went out of a deep love for children and a desire to bring joy to them during difficult times. He spent his own money on small gifts and balloons, which he gave wherever he went. The children loved to see him come, as did the parents and the hospital staff. He refused to tell anyone who he was. He was a truly happy man, not because of the honor he received, but because of the love he was able to share.

Sometimes it is easy to forget that the good feeling we receive from doing good is the greatest reward. Our egos get in the way, and we long for recognition when we do good things. When we diligently seek to do good, we procure the favor of God, and there is nothing greater we could ever hope to achieve. Jesus Christ came to this earth as a gift freely given from God. It was not deserved, but we are so thankful that it came. It is the same spirit of giving that God looks for in His children. When we have opportunities to give, we should do so with no thought of reward or recognition.

PRAYER: You have given so very much to me, Lord; now help me give of myself to others. I want to serve You with gladness and reflect the light of Your love to all the people I meet. Destroy my selfish spirit, and replace it with Your giving grace. Amen.

Pursuing Jesus

Whoso loveth instruction loveth knowledge:
but he that hateth reproof is brutish.
PROVERBS 12:1

Law school had seemed like a dream. The young woman had worked many years to get there, and now it was unreal. She never thought there could be so much work to do. She had given it everything she had, and now it was coming down to the last week of her last year. Her efforts paid off. She finished at the very top of her class, and she was lauded with honors. She looked around at many of her classmates. She knew how disappointed some of them had been with their own performances, but she couldn't really feel sorry for them. They had all had the same opportunities, and some used them well; others abused them. Each one got what they paid for. She loved to study and learn, and she received the benefits of her labor.

It is true of all of us that we will put forth the most effort to do the things we love most. We will give all we have to some cause or project that we love and believe in. Jesus Christ wants to be that cause in our lives. He wants us to pursue Him with everything we've got. If we will do that, we will know God, but if we follow some lesser god, then we will never know Him. It is good to listen to the Word of God and to seek Him in Scripture. By knowing God, we may have all the blessings that God can bestow, and we will rest in joy, eternally.

PRAYER: I want to seek You with every ounce of my being. Help me to devote myself wholly to You. Grace me with true knowledge, and lead me by Your instruction, O Lord. Amen.

LIVING BY LIES

The words of the wicked are to lie in wait for blood:
but the mouth of the upright shall deliver them.
The wicked are overthrown, and are not:
but the house of the righteous shall stand.
PROVERBS 12:6–7

When the pencil box disappeared, the little girl saw her chance. Going up to the teacher, she said, "I saw Timmy around the desk. He took the pencil box." The little girl had not liked Tim, and she felt that it would be great fun to get him into trouble. The teacher brought Timmy into the room and told the little girl to repeat her story. Timmy burst into tears and said, "That's not true. I never took anything!" The teacher sent Timmy home with a note for his parents, and she thanked the little girl for coming to her.

The next day, when the little girl arrived at school, the teacher was waiting with Timmy and another boy. "This boy came to me this morning and admitted taking the box. Why did you say Timmy did it?" Suddenly, the lie didn't seem like so much fun. The little girl never thought she might get caught.

There is only one outcome for people who live by the lie. They will have to answer for their actions before God. It is much better to always speak truth, for the mouth of the upright will indeed deliver them.

PRAYER: May my speech always be truthful and my words always uplift. Forbid that I should ever hurt anyone by careless speech or an unkind word. Grant that I might speak with Your grace and Your love at all times. Amen.

LEARNING ABOUT VALUE

He that tilleth his land shall be satisfied with bread:
but he that followeth vain persons is void of understanding.
PROVERBS 12:11

A member of my youth group complained because his father wouldn't let him have the car whenever he wanted it. "It's not fair." Actually, the young man had been told that if he was to drive the car, he had to help maintain it and keep it filled with gas. His father had never said that he couldn't use it. So often we take for granted the things which are not ours. We think we deserve things when we have no real claim to them at all. When we are forced to work for something, we appreciate it so much more. When things are just handed to us and we make no personal sacrifice, then we don't learn the true value of things.

We sometimes complain to God that we have to work too hard, or that we wish we had all the things we want, but if God freely granted all of our wishes, we would lose sight of how blessed we really are. When we have to work for something, then we know its value, and we stop taking things for granted. It is good for us to learn to appreciate what we do have and to quit dwelling on all the things we wish we could have instead.

PRAYER: O Lord, You have given me so very much. Thank You that it has not come too easily, but that I have had to put forth an effort to obtain it. I have been blessed in so many wonderful ways, and so I offer my thanks and my praise. Amen.

CONTROLLING ANGER

A fool's wrath is presently known:
but a prudent man covereth shame.
PROVERBS 12:16

The man impatiently looked at his watch. He was sure his friend had told him to be on this corner at five-thirty sharp. It was now ten until six, and he still had not shown up. The man grabbed his coat and briefcase and headed for home. All the way home he grew more and more angry. It was his birthday, and it had been tradition for him to meet his friend for coffee after work. They had done so for better than twenty years. He'd never been stood up before.

When he turned the corner and headed toward his driveway, he noticed the car of his friend parked in the driveway. Getting from the car, he slammed the door and stormed into the house. Seeing his friend, he flew into a rage. "Where were you? Some friend. You promised me that you'd pick me up. You lied to me!" The man's face was red with rage and hurt. So angered was he that he didn't notice the cake or the circle of friends who had waited to surprise him. An embarrassed hush settled over the entire group.

Anger can be a terrible thing. Everyone has the right to get angry, but it should never control us. We should be prudent and learn to hold our tongues so that we might not embarrass others and ourselves by our uncontrolled wrath.

PRAYER: Help me to think before I react, Father, that I might not cause grief or pain. Let me learn patience and control so that my actions may be a glory to You rather than a shame. Guide my actions and my words, Father. Amen.

HEART TO MOUTH

There is that speaketh like the piercings of a sword:
but the tongue of the wise is health.
The lip of truth shall be established for ever:
but a lying tongue is but for a moment.
PROVERBS 12:18–19

Words spoken in the heat of anger are spoken so quickly, but their impact goes so deep. Once said, words cannot be taken back. It seems to take many more words to heal than it does to hurt. It takes one unkind word to cut someone to the quick, but it may take a dozen apologies to make everything well again.

The words of our mouths are the reflections of our hearts. Like a fountain, we spring forth either good or foul water, depending on the source. If we keep Jesus Christ enthroned in our hearts, then we can rest assured that all of our words will be gracious, but if we continually take control of our lives back from Christ's loving hands, then we must take responsibility for words that may issue forth in anger or unkindness. Christ is willing to transform our hearts, to clean up the source of our life's fountain. When we give our lives to Christ, we allow Him to make us new. It is good to give our lives to Him daily, that we might always be reminded that He is the Lord and ruler of our hearts. With Christ in control, our words will be established forever, by the truth of Christ within.

PRAYER: Consecrate my life this day, O Lord. Make me new, inside and out. Please be the ruler of my heart, dear Jesus. I am nothing without Your spirit guiding from within. Shine through me, O Lord. Amen.

Knowing When to Speak

A prudent man concealeth knowledge:
but the heart of fools proclaimeth foolishness.
PROVERBS 12:23

There was a woman who thought she was the authority on every subject that came up. Whether it was asked for or not, the woman offered her opinion. No one else could finish a thought or sentence without her butting in to present her thoughts. Some people avoided her, but she didn't care. She always told herself that they were closed-minded and weren't worth her concern. She felt that her opinions were as good as gold, and she proclaimed them proudly. What she perceived to be great wisdom caused others to feel pity and embarrassment for her.

There are few things worse than a know-it-all. No one likes to have knowledge lorded over them. The person who talks the loudest and longest generally has the least to say. It is much better to watch carefully our words and learn to use them well and sparingly. We all have important things to say, and we all have a right to be heard, but we should be as interested in what others have to share as we are committed to our own thoughts. There is a saying, " 'Tis better to remain silent and appear a fool, than to speak and remove all doubt." Meant as a joke, perhaps, but there is a wisdom there that we all can learn from.

PRAYER: Make my words a blessing rather than a burden, Father. Grace my tongue with the ability to speak wisely and concisely, never being a bore, and help me to be ever mindful of the things other people might wish to share. Amen.

THE SQUIRRELS AND THE OPOSSUM

The slothful man roasteth not that which he took in hunting:
but the substance of a diligent man is precious.
PROVERBS 12:27

The squirrels worked diligently to lay aside stores for the winter. They moved from place to place, burying and storing their precious nuts. They worked from early in the morning until dusk. As they settled into their homes of sticks and leaves, two bright, beady eyes looked out from under the bushes.

An opossum poked its head out from the brush and sniffed at the air. It moved from hiding place to hiding place, uprooting and eating all of the squirrels' hard-earned stores. After it ransacked the lot, it returned to its home for a rest.

If you are a squirrel, the tactics of the possum are extremely hard to swallow. There are so many people in the world today who feel they should be entitled to something for nothing. They reap profit from the labors of others without a thought of gratitude or thanks. It is good to know that what is done in this earthly life is all seen by our Father in heaven. Nothing occurs that is outside of His knowledge. Those who receive their reward on earth by ill-gotten means will receive no reward in heaven. It is the diligent and devoted here on earth who are pleasing to the Lord and whom He will richly reward in heaven. Our reward lies ahead, and we will enjoy it eternally.

PRAYER: It is hard to work so hard to see so little gain, O God. Please give me patience and the strength to proceed. Keep my eyes set on the reward that lies ahead, not the riches that this world can offer. Amen.

Good Guys and Bad Guys

Righteousness keepeth him that is upright in the way:
but wickedness overthroweth the sinner.
PROVERBS 13:6

Old time Western movies had a magical appeal. Good and evil were clearly defined by the color of the hat. The bad guys always got theirs in the end, and the good guys battled unbelievable odds and always came out on top. There seemed to be something inherently wrong with the bad guys which tripped them up and led to their downfall. The good guys knew all the right moves and never made the same kinds of mistakes as the bad guys did. Righteousness would be rewarded and wickedness would be destroyed. People who loved Westerns loved them because there was such a basic sense of justice.

We all want justice. We need to believe that good will ultimately prevail and that evil will be destroyed once and for all. Christ did just that. Christ slammed the door on evil and ensured that good indeed would prevail. Through Christ's victory over death, sin was overthrown and death lost all power. Virtue and righteousness prevailed, sending forth a light that will never be extinguished. The Westerns had the right idea. The black hats don't stand a chance. The good guys have already won!

PRAYER: Lord, I praise Your victory over the grave and rejoice that death has been destroyed for all time. Sin has no lasting power because You have washed me clean in the blood of Christ. I thank You, and I praise Your holy name, for giving me such a precious and lasting gift. Amen.

BURNING BRIGHTLY

The light of the righteous rejoiceth:
but the lamp of the wicked shall be put out.
PROVERBS 13:9

Two roommates prepared for finals. One had been diligent all through the semester and had studied every night. The other had floated through classes, doing very little work throughout the semester. As finals approached, the first student was relaxed and reviewed quickly and quietly. The other roommate found that he was lost, buried beneath a mountain of work too high to climb in the small amount of time left. The first student studied normal hours, then got plenty of rest and was fresh for the exams. The other student studied late into the night, burning the midnight oil, and found himself exhausted as the testing began.

When we do the things we know we should, and we face up to our responsibilities, we find that they aren't really such a burden at all. When we shirk our duties, however, we find that they can become too much for us to handle. That light which burns within each one of us burns most brightly when we do the things we should. When we avoid doing what is right, the light flickers and dims. Righteousness fuels the fire. Wickedness works to snuff it out. The choice is ours. We can burn brightly, shining forth with the light of Christ, or we can shine weakly, in danger of going out at any moment.

PRAYER: Let my light shine forth brightly, Lord. Feed the fire that burns within my breast. Make it a beacon of Your love for the entire world to see. Help me to shine without flickering or fading. Amen.

OBTAINING WEALTH

Wealth gotten by vanity shall be diminished:
but he that gathereth by labour shall increase.
PROVERBS 13:11

A successful actress had made millions on her looks alone. Her face had graced the pages of a hundred ads, and she appeared on television and in movies regularly. She received as much as sixty thousand dollars for an episode of a regular series on television. Everything seemed to be going well until an accident scarred her, and she was no longer in demand. Though she had made millions, she had spent millions just as fast. She left acting a poor and bitter woman.

We often envy the life of stars. We believe that they have everything a person could want and that their lives are somehow magical. There is magic in the lives of stars, but it is not all good. Some of the magic is "here today, gone tomorrow." Nothing is permanent, and the big money they make is gone with nothing to show for it.

It is good to be satisfied with what we receive for the labors we pursue. What we receive as wages for the work we do is money well received and deserved. We can be proud of the fact that we work hard for our money. It is right that we should receive gain for the effort we put forth. God rewards those who are steadfast in their labors. Those who receive wealth for their vanities have already received their reward.

PRAYER: Make me steadfast in my endeavors, O Lord. Keep my eyes set on my labors, and bless all my efforts. Let me feel the joy and contentment that honest labor brings, almighty God. Amen.

THE WORD OF GOD

Whoso despiseth the word shall be destroyed:
but he that feareth the commandment shall be rewarded.

PROVERBS 13:13

The woman sat at her desk reading the Bible over her lunch hour. One of her associates came up to her and said, "You don't really believe that garbage, do you? That's for weirdos and Jesus freaks." The woman looked up at the young man and said, "Have you ever read it? Do you know what it really says?"

"Hey, I don't have time to waste. You go on and read your fairy tales. I'll stick to reality."

"What happens if this is reality?" she asked, holding up the Bible.

"I'll worry about that when the time comes," he replied.

The time for a decision like that is now. If people reject the opportunity to read the Scriptures and do not come to know the truth of Christ, then they will not get a second chance. Anyone who despises the Word of God will have no place with God in the final times. It is the person who reads the Bible and lives his life accordingly, who will receive the reward of life everlasting. There is no greater book in existence, and it behooves each person to take its contents very seriously. Only a foolish person criticizes something that he or she has never read. It is the prudent person who makes time to investigate, then draws a conclusion based on what he has experienced.

PRAYER: You have become real to me through the reading of Your Word. Assist me as I attempt to spread Your Word and bring others to the threshold of Your truth contained in the Old and New Testaments. Bless this effort. Amen.

New Ideas

*Poverty and shame shall be to him that refuseth instruction:
but he that regardeth reproof shall be honoured.*
PROVERBS 13:18

A man who was very successful in business was asked what his secret was. He answered, "I never think I know everything. I'm always ready to listen to a new idea, and I always want to know when I'm doing something wrong." For forty years he had been a top financial consultant, and he had a reputation for listening to even the youngest of colleagues. He never defended himself when his superiors rebuked him. He merely listened to the comment, then did his best to improve.

This is the kind of spirit God wants in His children. God wants each one of us to grow to our full potential. Jesus tells us that we should be perfect as God Himself is perfect. The only way we can hope to move in that direction is to open ourselves to the constructive comments and criticisms of others. People can see things in us that we might miss ourselves. Having the integrity and wisdom to seek out the counsel of others shows a definite desire to grow. We can do little else that is so pleasing to God. Only a fool refuses to listen to the observations of others. That person is too insecure to listen and too self-centered to want to grow.

PRAYER: Dear heavenly Father, bless me that I might grow to my full potential. Inspire me by Your Word and by the example of Your Son, Jesus Christ. Fill me with Your Spirit so that I may more closely resemble You in all that I do. Amen.

FIGHTING INJUSTICE

Much food is in the tillage of the poor:
but there is that is destroyed for want of judgment.
PROVERBS 13:23

The farmland was rich in minerals, and its produce was bountiful. The farm workers labored long and hard, and through their efforts, the yield was high. Unfortunately, the laborers received little recompense for their hard work. The farm was owned by a large corporation, and the residents were all hired by the farm at low wages. Their land was taken from them, and they in turn were made slaves to it. Most of the farm workers were on the verge of starvation, while they worked in the plentiful fields each day. The injustice of it all was incredible, but true. Their land was some of the most fertile in the world, but they were among the poorest of people.

Injustice should touch us at the very root of our souls. That part of us which is in God's image should be enraged by the unfairness in our world. And it should be the Christ in us that compels us to try to fight injustice wherever we see it. We may not be rich or powerful, but we do control our actions and our resources. We have the ability to refuse to support others who would take advantage of the poor. We can speak out against injustice, and we can offer comfort to anyone who is persecuted. When we do this, we have the joy of our heavenly Father.

PRAYER: Ours is a world of great injustice and inequality. Please guide me that I might work to change the way things are. Open my eyes to the plight of the poor, and lead me in the ways that I might combat it. Amen.

LEARNING TO BE CONTENT

The righteous eateth to the satisfying of his soul:
but the belly of the wicked shall want.
PROVERBS 13:25

Two men had been friends throughout their lives. One man was extremely wealthy, having accumulated great riches throughout his life. The other man was well off, but he could hardly be considered wealthy. The rich man asked his friend, "Why is it you have so much less than I do, but you appear to be so much happier?"

His friend replied, "I've always been content with what I have. You, on the other hand, have set one goal after another. Once you attain one goal, you set one higher. I've always had everything I wanted and lacked nothing. You've never been satisfied with what you have, but always want more."

When we look at what we have and are thankful for it, we find that we are fulfilled; but when we are always longing for the things we do not have, then we find ourselves in want, and we cannot be happy. The wise person looks not at what he does not have, but he concentrates on what is his. The fool ignores the blessings he has been given, and focuses on the things he wishes he could own. So long as we look at the things we do not have, we can never be satisfied, but if we will be content with what we have, then we will never have to know want. God has given graciously to us all. It is right to thank Him for His great gifts.

PRAYER: O Lord, I cannot believe how much I have. I cannot thank You enough for all You have given me. Help me to remember that true wealth is not measured by what I own, but by the joy that You have put into my life. Amen.

AN OPEN MIND

A scorner seeketh wisdom, and findeth it not:
but knowledge is easy unto him that understandeth.
PROVERBS 14:6

A girl sat in the circle of the Bible study and listened to the lesson being taught. When asked what she thought, she replied, "This is stupid." She folded her arms across her chest and leaned back in her chair. She tuned out the rest of the lesson, and afterward she vowed never to return. A friend of hers said that she was being closed-minded, but she said, "I don't have time for this junk. I want to know how to live better, just like everybody else, but I don't think this helps at all." The girl never gave the group a second chance.

It is interesting how some people can find the answers they are seeking in churches, while others seem unaffected. Partially, it has to do with the attitude we come with. If we are open to God and are willing to give Him a chance to disclose Himself, we will find Him. But if we come skeptically, and we scorn His power to change lives, then we block His effectiveness. For every attempt He makes to reach us, we come up with some excuse to explain it away, and we come away as empty as when we arrived. If we come before God unwilling to listen to His Word, then we will never find wisdom, but when we are open-minded and willing to hear, God will grant us the knowledge we so desire.

PRAYER: I come before You with an open heart and an open mind. Grant that I might have knowledge that passes human understanding. Guard me from doubt and disbelief. Open my eyes to Your truth. Amen.

My Heart Friend

The heart knoweth his own bitterness;
and a stranger doth not intermeddle with his joy.

PROVERBS 14:10

The woman was in shock at the death of her husband. They had been married for fifteen years, and she had settled into the idea that they would be together forever. She couldn't quite believe that it was true. Every once in awhile she would walk through the house just to make sure he wasn't there somewhere.

Her friends had been so kind and helpful, but she was glad they were gone now. She thought if she heard one more person tell her they knew exactly how she felt, she would scream. They didn't know. They couldn't. Somehow it was different. She'd said the same thing on a number of occasions, but never again. It didn't do anything to help. Her pain was her own, and there was no way that anyone could share it.

It is good to have friends that care, but we can have no friend greater than Jesus Christ. Christ dwells within our hearts, and so He is the only one Who can honestly comfort us when our hearts are broken. Christ is as close to us as we are to ourselves. He is a part of us, and when we suffer, He suffers, but when we rejoice, He rejoices with us. We are one with Christ, and it is so good to know that we never have to face life alone. He is with us in good times and bad, and He will never leave us.

PRAYER: Christ Jesus, You know me to the very depth of my being. Dwell within my heart, and grace it with Your strength and love. Let me feel Your presence within me. Guide me, protect me, stay with me, I pray. Amen.

Artificial Happiness

Even in laughter the heart is sorrowful;
and the end of that mirth is heaviness.
PROVERBS 14:13

She hated closing time at the bar. The crowds had thinned and the lights were unplugged, and everything quieted down. It got too quiet. She had to face the thought of going back to her lonely apartment. She came to the bar to melt into the noise and laughter. She could be charming in the right setting. She could at least have a good time for a few hours, but it always came to an abrupt end, and she had to face her desperate unhappiness. She sometimes wished she could find a party that never ended, but that was senseless. Eventually she would have to come back to reality, and her problems would all be waiting for her when she did.

So many of our attempts to find happiness end in futility. We look in all the wrong places for fulfillment and happiness. We exert such energy pursuing good things, and we never attain them. The deep loneliness that we sometimes feel inside is homesickness for our Creator and heavenly home. When we take Christ into our hearts, we never have to face the loneliness that destroys. We stop looking for artificial answers, and we focus our attention on the one real answer: God. In Him we find fulfillment and life.

PRAYER: O God, You have given my life such meaning. I no longer seek other answers, for I have found the one true answer. In Christ, I have found everything I could ever desire. Thank You, O Lord. Amen.

SELF-CONTROL

A wise man feareth, and departeth from evil:
but the fool rageth, and is confident.
He that is soon angry dealeth foolishly:
and a man of wicked devices is hated.
PROVERBS 14:16–17

The two players sat transfixed, their entire concentration on the chessboard in front of them. The match had gone on for over an hour, and the heat was rising. Both players were looking for blood. They had played masterfully. Then, as quickly as it had started, it was over. A single wrong move resulted in defeat. The loser stood up abruptly and wiped out the table. He stormed to the side of the room and slammed his hand into the wall, breaking bones and tearing the skin. He cried out in pain and rage and yelled for the room to be cleared. When the storm subsided, he sat alone in pain and shame, not only from his defeat, but also from his childish display.

Self-control is an important part of the Christian's life. Christ had many occasions when He could have lost control and wreaked havoc on His enemies. That would have destroyed His mission on earth: to teach love and provide an example for how we should live our lives. Anger is a natural reaction, but it cannot be allowed to take control of us. When we live by our passions, we live on the danger line, and eventually we will fall prey to sin. The wise person learns to respect the power of his emotions, and he departs from situations where he might lose control.

PRAYER: O almighty God, save me from myself. When anger rises within my heart, help me to control it and channel it in constructive ways. Do not let me be a captive to my passions. Amen.

WRONG JUDGMENT

The poor is hated even of his own neighbour:
but the rich hath many friends.
PROVERBS 14:20

I had a friend who got along wonderfully with me when we were alone, but when his other friends were with us, he treated me as if I were beneath him. He was wealthy, and so were many of his friends. They had their own language, and they judged people by what they owned, what they wore, and what they drove. One day, in frustration, I told my friend that either he could treat me the same way no matter who we were with, or he could forget having me as a friend. To my surprise, he chose to end the friendship.

It is amazing how we find ways to judge one another. We set standards for acceptability and draw lines defining what is good enough and what isn't. We categorize people and force them into molds. This is wrong. We do our neighbor an injustice when we judge him. We are all children of God, and it is our purpose to see the face of Christ in all our brothers and sisters. When we treat another person as an inferior, it is as if we are doing it to Christ. Jesus taught us to love all people, regardless of their status. We are to accept everyone just as they are. When we learn to do that, we begin to love our neighbors as God loves us.

PRAYER: *Make me love everyone equally, O Lord. Help me to accept all people just as they are. Help me to see my brothers and sisters as You see them, through eyes of unconditional love. Amen.*

EMPTY PROMISES

In all labour there is profit:
but the talk of the lips tendeth only to penury.
PROVERBS 14:23

The politician promised so many wonderful things. His constituents wanted to put their faith in him. They kept hoping someone would come along who cared about their plight. Every time new promises were made, the hopes of the people soared. Each time, though, their hopes were dashed to the ground as the great talk dissolved into just so much wind. This time they hoped it would be different. They had to hold onto something. Promises were the best they could find. If even half the talk resulted in action, they would be a great deal better off than they were now.

Talk without action can be destructive. If we make a promise, we must be committed to following through. Jesus told the people of His day that they should not swear, because when they didn't do what they said, it was a sin. It is good for us to commit ourselves to helping other people, but when we make empty promises, we are being cruel and unloving. It is through action that we show how much we care, not through mere words. Actions speak louder than words, and actions done in love speak the truth of Christ in our lives. Let us always strive to follow the example of Christ, saving our words until we are ready to act.

PRAYER: You have given me so much, O Lord; let me now share it with those who need it. Let not my words be a trap for me, but let me act in a way pleasing to You. There is nothing that needs to be said; only love needs to be shown. Amen.

THE PRISONER

In the fear of the LORD is strong confidence:
and his children shall have a place of refuge.
The fear of the LORD is a fountain of life,
to depart from the snares of death.

PROVERBS 14:26–27

A young Russian was arrested for smuggling Bibles into area prisons. He stood before a tribunal for sentencing, and they shipped him off to a high-security prison. Each day, he was taken to a warden who asked him if he was sorry for what he had done. His answer was always the same. Each time he said no, he was beaten, then returned to his cell. Years went by, and the daily routine continued. The Russian prison officials hoped to break the spirit of the young man, but instead, an interesting thing happened. The prisoner helped thousands of prisoners, and over time, many of them were converted. Within the prison a great revival took place, all because the young man refused to renounce his faith in Christ.

The story is a familiar one. Christians have been persecuted over the centuries. When they withstood the torture and torment, they proved to be powerful witnesses to the truth of Christ. A good knowledge of God gives us confidence so strong that nothing can shake it. The truth of God is a fountain of life, and by dwelling within it, we depart from sin and all its ramifications. When we stand fast in the truth of God, He will give us everything we need to hold on.

PRAYER: Be with me, God, to guide me, to support me, to strengthen and love me. Never depart from me, Lord, that I might stand fast in the face of every trial and persecution. Allow me to be an example for others. Amen.

HELPING THOSE IN NEED

He that oppresseth the poor reproacheth his Maker;
but he that honoureth him hath mercy on the poor.
PROVERBS 14:31

A couple walked along a darkened street and came upon a young woman sitting with a baby in her arms. As they passed, the young woman held forth a hand and asked for some small gift to help her feed her baby. The couple recoiled from the girl's hand, and they hurried on their way. As they strolled along, they realized that they were not alone. Another person followed them. They quickened their pace, but the figure stayed right behind them. Finally, in frustration and fear, the man turned to the stranger and asked him what he wanted. The stranger replied, "You have had the chance to feed the Son of God, and you have turned away. Therefore, if you would hope to come into God's glory, do not be surprised if He turns from you." With that, the stranger walked away, leaving the couple to stare in disbelief.

Christ said that when we help others who are in need, it is the same as doing it for Him. All of God's children were created in His image. When we reject any one of God's children, it is as if we are rejecting Him. He wants us to give from our abundance to make life more comfortable for one another. When we see the world through the eyes of God, we have compassion on the poor and suffering, and it becomes our heart's desire to help them.

PRAYER: You have put me here with a purpose, O Lord, and it is to learn to serve You. I can best serve You by meeting the needs of those I see in need around me. Grant that I might never turn away from someone in need. Amen.

OUR WATCHMAN

The eyes of the LORD are in every place,
beholding the evil and the good.
PROVERBS 15:3

The corporate offices of a large company had a wonderful record for security. In its twenty-five-year history, there had never been a break-in. There had been attempts, but the intruders were always apprehended before they could make a move. The secret to the fine security record was a high-technology video center which allowed a watchman to keep tabs on all key entry points to the building. By sitting in a chair surrounded by monitors, the watchman could see the entire plant. Nothing could happen without the guard being immediately notified.

God is like that watchman. There is nothing that occurs that God is not immediately aware of. No matter how insignificant an act may seem, it does not escape the notice of the Lord. His eye watches everyone: the good, the evil, the young, the old, male, female, black, white, red, yellow—every person who lives upon this earth is in God's loving sight. It is comforting to know that He sees us in the good times and the bad and that He knows exactly what is going on. He can share in the innermost thoughts we have, and He knows our desires before we even express them. God knows us, and He loves us, totally.

PRAYER: Keep Your eye upon me, Lord. Watch my comings and goings, and be with me in everything I do. Bless my actions, and keep me protected by Your loving care. Help me to do the things which are most pleasing in Your sight. Amen.

In God's Sight

Hell and destruction are before the LORD:
how much more then the hearts of the children of men?
PROVERBS 15:11

A light plane crashed in the desert. The pilot survived the crash and began a long, hot trek toward civilization. He wandered for hours without seeing anything remotely man-made. As day turned to night, he began to think he had survived the crash just to die a slow, painful death. With morning light, he set out once more in search of rescue. When his last ounce of strength gave out, he sat down and began to cry. His sobs grew in intensity, and they merged with another sound. Controlling his emotions, he looked up to see a jeep approaching in the distance. He bowed his head to say a quick thank-you, then waved to the driver of the vehicle.

There are times when we feel that we must surely be out of God's sight, or at least out of His favor. It is comforting to know that God sees everything that goes on no matter where it is. God can see into the very depths of hell, so it is no great wonder that He can see into our hearts to know what we are feeling and thinking. Our lives are open to our Creator, and at the time when we think we have no hope, the grace of the Lord will reach down to us and let us know that we are saved. God will never leave us, no matter how far we may go.

PRAYER: Be with me, Father, as I walk along the many paths which make up my life. When I lose my way and turn from the one true path, wait patiently for me to return, and keep me ever in Your watchful eye. Amen.

DECIDE TO BE HAPPY

A merry heart maketh a cheerful countenance:
but by sorrow of the heart the spirit is broken.
PROVERBS 15:13

You never get mad. You always seem to be happy and having a good time. I don't understand it. I wish I could be like you." The two walked along the beach together.

"It's really not that hard. You just have to decide that you're going to be happy, then do it. I got tired of being unhappy about everything, so I decided to quit," the other answered.

"It can't be that easy. There has to be more to it."

"It was that easy for me. I just thought about which I liked better: being happy or being sad. I don't like being sad, so I fight it."

We can decide to be happy. It takes work, but it is a conscious effort that anyone can make. God is the giver of the greatest joy a person can ever know. When we make Him the Lord of our lives, He can work within us to fill us with this unspeakable joy. All we need to do is ask Him in. When we are filled with sorrow, we break the spirit, and we undercut the effectiveness of Christ in our lives. The Lord dwells in joy, and He is well at home in a heart that is happy. When we are truly filled with joy, the whole world can see it. They will notice that we are not like everyone else, and there is no more powerful testimony to the power of God than a smile that cannot be taken away.

PRAYER: Fill my heart with Your joy, O Lord. Change the light of my countenance to happiness so that everyone will know the effect You have had on my life. Wherever I go, help me to spread joy and love. I praise You for Your gracious gift. Amen.

SET YOUR SIGHTS ON GOD

Better is little with the fear of the LORD,
than great treasure and trouble therewith.
PROVERBS 15:16

She had always dreamed of what it would be like to be rich. She had never really been poor, but the idea of having a lot of money had always been exciting. Now it was reality. Her father had died, and all of his wealth was hers. She didn't understand half of what the lawyers had said about taxes and trusts, but she knew she was rich. Already people were calling her and sending her literature about boats and cars and homes. People she hadn't seen in years were showing up from everywhere. She was a little afraid of strangers who came around. Her friend told her that people would be more likely to break into her home to steal from her now. She wondered if she would ever get out from under all the red tape so that she could start living it up.

The minute we begin turning our attention to wealth and possessions, we turn it from the Lord. The less we own, the less we are distracted. The poor person can deal with God continually, but the rich person has to attend to other things. God wants to be the sole possessor of our hearts. He will not share our hearts with any other god. We all must make the choice concerning what we will pursue. The wise person chooses to pursue the Lord.

PRAYER: Almighty God, there are so many things that pull at my attention. I am blinded by the glitter of wealth and glamour. Shade my eyes in the shadow of Your divine Spirit. Guard me from the traps of the world. Amen.

A Lazy Body

*The way of the slothful man is as an hedge of thorns:
but the way of the righteous is made plain.*
PROVERBS 15:19

I t was maddening to try to get the children to do their work. Whenever there was a game or an activity, they were ready, willing, and able. But at those times when the chores needed to be done, they were nowhere to be found. They were getting lazy, and it was annoying. It was also troubling to have to punish and threaten in order to get them motivated. They should want to pitch in. They lived in the same house, and everyone had to pull their weight, or it just wasn't fair.

The same is true in the body of Christ. In the body there are many parts, and each one must do what it was created for, or the body cannot function as well. It is important that we always give our best effort. Anything less is an insult to our Creator. We shine a negative light onto God when we are lazy or slothful. Christians should be proud to do their best in all things, as a sign to others that being a Christian is what we are most often judged by. If our actions are positive, then our testimony to God is a positive one, but if our actions are unbecoming, then we shame God, and we give people a bad impression of what it means to be a Christian.

PRAYER: During the times when I get lazy, help me remember that my actions reflect not only upon myself but also upon You, O Lord, and upon all others who call themselves Christian. Help me to always put forth the best image possible. Amen.

A Job Well Done

A man hath joy by the answer of his mouth:
and a word spoken in due season, how good is it!
PROVERBS 15:23

The algebra problem was a tough one. No one had given the right answer yet, and the teacher had gone through half the class. Andrea hoped that the teacher wouldn't get to her. She wasn't sure her answer was even close. Smarter people than she had missed it. The most she could hope for was that someone else would get the answer before the teacher got to her. Her heart sank, and she felt her cheeks flush as the teacher called her name. Timidly, she offered her answer. To her delight, the teacher praised her for getting the right answer. Andrea felt a surge of pride at her accomplishment.

It is a joy when we know we have done a job and that we have done it well. When we say or do the right thing, it makes us feel good. That is why God wants us to always do what is right. When we live a life of righteousness, then that good feeling never leaves us. We experience not only the joy of a job well done, but we provide a good example for other people to see. God is proud of us when we do what is right and good. We can feel great peace knowing that we are doing what God hopes we will do. His favor is worth more than all the riches of the earth.

PRAYER: I pray that my words may always be full of grace and pleasing to You. When I proclaim Your greatness and spread Your word, I do what is pleasing in Your sight. Help me that I might forever do what You want me to. Amen.

A Shine from Within

The light of the eyes rejoiceth the heart:
and a good report maketh the bones fat.

PROVERBS 15:30

Their grandfather had looked so bad, so frail, the last time they had seen him. They remembered their grandpa as a happy man who had loved to spend his time with his family. He gave so much of himself, and they loved him. He had always been so much fun to be with. It was terribly painful to see him lying in a hospital bed so pathetically. If he had to die, it would be better for him to go quickly. The thought of seeing him waste away was too painful to deal with.

When they arrived at the hospital, they went right to his room. When they opened the door, he was sitting up in bed. He turned to look at them, and joy came into his face. A sparkle gleamed in his eye, and his granddaughter realized that that gleam was what had been missing before. Just seeing that sparkle gave her a feeling of peace. Seeing him this way, she knew he would be all right.

There is something about truly good people which shines forth from within. When we are in the presence of goodness, we feel it. Something deep inside of us responds to that spirit which emanates outward, and we feel wonderful. That something special is God's love, and it cannot be contained once it fills a human heart.

PRAYER: May the joy and peace of my relationship with You show from my face and shine forth from my body. I want everyone to know that I am Yours, and that You make all the difference in the world. Amen.

CONCEITED HONOR

The fear of the LORD is the instruction of wisdom;
and before honour is humility.
PROVERBS 15:33

There was an actor who was fond of telling everyone how wonderful he was. His house was a museum of memorabilia from his career. His rave reviews were framed and hung in every room. Awards graced shelves and tables, and copies of his movies were played on videotape machines on large screens whenever visitors came by. He took such delight in rattling off his achievements that no one else ever felt compelled to praise him.

Too often, people seek after honors when they should be striving after humility. Honors are not something that we deserve. They are gifts, and should be given by others, not by ourselves. Conceit is a sin, and when we praise our own efforts we slip into conceit. God is most pleased when we commit ourselves to doing what is right. Even if no honors come to us in this life, God will honor us richly in the life to come. It is the humble man or woman who is able to keep sights set on God and doing His will. If we will use our time doing the things that God has asked of us, we will not have time to brag about our accomplishments. God has given us plenty to keep us busy all the days of our lives. If we stay committed to doing what is pleasing in His sight, He will bless us all of our days.

PRAYER: Keep me humble, Lord. Help me to remember that I am nothing without You. You have given me everything I have and everything I am. You have blessed me with so many wonderful things, and I praise You. Amen.

GOD'S CHILDREN

The LORD hath made all things for himself:
yea, even the wicked for the day of evil.
PROVERBS 16:4

S he had to be the most forgiving woman in the world. Three young hoodlums had broken into her house, had tied her up, stolen all her valuables, and she didn't even have a harsh word to say about them. She said, "I'm fine, and that's all that really matters. Those boys are God's children just like everyone else. They have just gone bad. God will take care of them, so I don't have to worry about it one bit."

It is difficult to let go of bad feelings that we hold against other people. When we have been wronged, we want justice done. We want to see the persecutors punished. Often we forget that they are children of God and that we must love even those who do not love us. Jesus said that if we love only those who are good and kind, we do not know the real meaning of love. It is when we can learn to love those who hate us and try to harm us that we can understand what love is all about. If God loved only those who were worthy of His love, then He would never love anyone. Love isn't something earned. It is something freely given, and God expects us to love everyone at least as much as we love ourselves. God created everything on this earth, and it is our duty to respect and honor His whole creation.

PRAYER: Most holy God, it is not easy to love those people who seem evil and try to hurt me. I get angry when people try to hurt me. I get angry when people try to take advantage of me. Help me to love with Your love, and to see life through Your eyes. Amen.

WHAT MONEY CAN'T DO

Better is a little with righteousness
than great revenues without right.
PROVERBS 16:8

It hadn't always been like this. When he had first started in business, he could sleep like a baby. He didn't have a care in the world. Now it was different. He tossed and turned every night because of the guilt he felt. He was short-tempered and angry all the time. He felt like a heel every time he foreclosed a mortgage. He had worked so long to get where he was, but there was no satisfaction in it, only turmoil. All the money and prestige in the world wouldn't make up for what he was feeling inside. He decided that the only way to deal with it was to quit his job. It was the best decision he ever made.

Sometimes we feel like money will make everything all right. We think that it can cure all our ills and make us whole. There are some things that money cannot do. It cannot give us peace of mind, and it cannot replace human relationships. We need other people, and we must love them more than money. When we serve money instead of people, we lose our sense of all that is right and good. It is much better to have little money and great happiness than to have mountains of money and no peace of mind.

PRAYER: Lord, I have what I need. Please make me content with that so that I don't go running off, pursuing things I do not need. Make me content with my life as it is, keeping me from dreaming of things that are really unimportant. Amen.

SPRING RAIN

In the light of the king's countenance is life;
and his favour is as a cloud of the latter rain.
PROVERBS 16:15

The planting was all done. The soil had been prepared, the seed had been laid, the fertilizer spread. Now all that was left to do was wait. If the rains came soon, everything would be all right, but if they held off just a week or two, it could greatly hurt the crop. The early spring rain was vital. A soft, steady rain could mean the difference between solvency and bankruptcy. The sky was full of deep gray clouds, rolling overhead. With the sound of distant thunder, the farmers breathed a deep sigh of relief.

It is hard to accept that our ultimate fate is in the hands of another. Even as great as God is, it is frightening to know that He holds our destiny in His hands. But just as the farmers feel relief at the first sign of rain, we can feel relieved that our fate has already been sealed by the blood of the Lamb, Jesus Christ. Through His sacrifice, we have been bonded to God. When we accept Christ into our lives, we accept the promise of eternal bliss with our Father in heaven. There can be no greater joy than knowing that God's love has saved us and that our future has been decided by His grace.

PRAYER: I look to You for my salvation, Lord, and I feel joy at the assurance of Your great love for me. I have done nothing that is deserving of Your favor, but I praise You from the very depths of my soul that You have looked upon me with compassion. Be with me now and each day to come. Amen.

WORKING WITH GOD

He that handleth a matter wisely shall find good:
and whoso trusteth in the LORD, happy is he.

PROVERBS 16:20

A teacher was highly respected for her ability to handle tough situations. Children never seemed to give her a hard time, and if they got out of line, she handled the matter quickly and decisively. Most of the children loved her, and their parents thought she was great. Her classes received good marks, and her pupils displayed much promise. The woman knew how to draw out the best from every student she taught. When asked about her ability to deal with children, she replied, "I pray for each one of them. I may not always know the best way to handle a situation, but God does, and the two of us working together can't miss. I know that He will lead me to do what is best for the kids. I know that with all my heart."

It is wonderful to be able to put all our trust in God. If we will let Him in on all the concerns of our lives, He will share in them and guide us through them. There is great power in prayer. When we pray to God, we make our concerns His concerns. We may be able to handle situations well, but we can handle them much better if we will ask God's help when we face them. True happiness comes to us when we can be confident that our decisions are sound, and that conviction can be ours if we will only turn to the Lord.

PRAYER: I want to put all of my trust in You, Father. Your wisdom is beyond my comprehension, and I know that You will always do what is best. Be with me when I make decisions, and guide my actions. Amen.

TRUE UNDERSTANDING

Understanding is a wellspring of life unto him that hath it:
but the instruction of fools is folly.
PROVERBS 16:22

The little girl had been told a thousand times not to play too near the street. She had never known why her parents were so firm about it, but she tried always to remember that it was forbidden. Once she had played too close, and her father had given her a spanking. She remembered that for a long time. It crossed her mind every once in awhile that she should try to find out what was so bad about the road, but she knew that she would have to go to the road to do it, and she wasn't ready to risk it. While she was thinking about the road, the neighbor's dog bolted out after a car. The driver hit his brakes and screeched to a halt, but it was too late. The dog had been hit and was dead. The little girl watched wide-eyed, and suddenly she understood what she had been told all of her life.

Many times we question the things we have been told. We don't understand why they are important. But when we understand the request and see the logic of it, then it isn't so hard to follow the instructions. Through understanding comes life. When we refuse to listen to the instructions of God in our lives, we are flirting with disaster. All He has commanded is for our safety and well-being. If we will listen to the word of God, a long and happy life will be ours.

PRAYER: O Lord, I do not understand everything You tell me, but I am trying, and I trust that You know what is best. Help me to be an obedient child, and help me to understand the ways You ask me to live. Amen.

DIGGING FOR EVIL

An ungodly man diggeth up evil:
and in his lips there is as a burning fire.
PROVERBS 16:27

He knew he would find it if he looked long enough. His opponent could not be the saint he painted himself to be. Every man had a skeleton in his closet. They were unavoidable in politics. Once the public knew he had been treated for drug abuse in college, his pure reputation would be tarnished, and he would be brought back to earth. It didn't matter that it had happened thirty years in the past. All that mattered was that it had happened. It was all he needed to drag his opponent's name through the dirt.

It is sad that so many people take pleasure in the pain they can cause. God wants us to devote as much of ourselves as possible to loving other people, not destroying them. There is nothing good that comes from spreading rumors and trying to discredit those around us. When we live in the past, and in the memory of sins gone by, we are chained to this existence, and we cannot move forward. Thankfully, God forgives us for the things we have done, and we can carry on with a clean slate. It is our duty to do the same for other people. If we hold the past against them, then we judge them unfairly. It is better to see each person for who he is now, and to realize that he, too, has been created in the image of God.

PRAYER: It takes so little to make others feel good, Father, and yet I don't try nearly enough. Make sure that I not only avoid doing harm, but also make me do good whenever and wherever possible. Amen.

THE DISCIPLINED PERSON

He that is slow to anger is better than the mighty;
and he that ruleth his spirit than he that taketh a city.
PROVERBS 16:32

The choice came down to two salesmen. The first got great results, but he was a little bit wild, and he couldn't always be counted on. The second man got average results, but he could be counted on every time. The account was important, and they really wanted the best person to go after it. The first man figured he would be selected, while the other man only hoped. It came as a surprise to them both when the second man was selected. It was decided that dependability was more important than a smooth come-on.

If we learn to practice self-control, we are well on the road to wisdom. God requires His followers to be disciplined. It is not always easy to be a Christian, but we are expected to hold fast to the faith through bad times as well as good. The disciplined person learns to deal with hardship and through discipline gains endurance. God loves the person who is steadfast and unyielding in faith. The person who gives up easily and forgets his trust has no place with God. We need to pray for strength in our faith, and trust that God will grant it. Discipline is greater than strength or intelligence or charm. It gives us the foundation we need to build a faith that cannot be shaken.

PRAYER: Give me a faith that will never fail, O Lord. I put my trust in You, because there is nothing on earth that is more powerful than Your might. Be with me to strengthen me and give me peace. Amen.

Helping the Poor

Whoso mocketh the poor reproacheth his Maker:
and he that is glad at calamities shall not be unpunished.
PROVERBS 17:5

The girls walked up the sidewalk to the next house. They had been collecting for hunger relief all afternoon, and they had done pretty well. They knocked at the door, and a man answered.

"We're collecting for the starving children in Calcutta. Could you give something?" one of the girls asked.

"No, I won't give anything. I don't care about the poor in Calcutta. If they want to eat, let them work like I do. If they can't get off their tails and earn a living, then they can go right ahead and starve."

With that, the man slammed the door in the faces of the stunned girls.

Whether we realize it or not, poor people are our responsibility. God has given us all the same charge: to love our neighbor as we love ourselves. When we know that someone is in need and we turn our heads so as not to be bothered, we take responsibility for the suffering of others. Those who intentionally cause another grief shall be punished by God Himself. God's people care for each other, and if we call ourselves children of God, yet we ignore those who are in need, then we are liars, and God will have no part in us. The choice is always ours.

PRAYER: Do not let me ignore my responsibility to other people who are in need. Help me to learn to be compassionate and caring. Let me use the excess from the abundance You have given me to ease the plight of the poor. Amen.

TRUE FORGIVENESS

He that covereth a transgression seeketh love;
but he that repeateth a matter separateth very friends.
PROVERBS 17:9

"You never let me forget, do you? Look, I said I was sorry a hundred times. I lied; I was wrong. It won't ever happen again!"

It happened every time they got into an argument. Josh knew he had done wrong, but he had asked forgiveness a dozen times. It would cool down, but then somehow it would come up and start another argument. If only Rick would let go of it, but no, he always held it over Josh's head. It hurt Josh to know that he wasn't forgiven. He had blown it and was truly sorry, but to be reminded of it over and over made him feel like a heel. He didn't know how much longer he could hear about it before it would begin to affect the two mens' friendship.

True forgiveness occurs only when we treat the subject as a closed matter. If we bring up old hurts whenever feelings fly, then we have never really forgiven. To hold a grudge is to build a wall between yourself and another person. Forgiveness breaks down walls. Christ came to break down walls and lead people to reconciliation. Before true healing can occur, though, we must let loose all old hurts and start fresh. Forgiveness gives us the clean start we need to heal all wounds. With God's help, we can grow closer than ever before.

PRAYER: Teach me how to drop old hurts into the sea of forget-fulness and truly forgive those who have harmed me. Fill me with Your grace, that I might learn how to be graceful to others. Amen.

EVIL FOR GOOD

Whoso rewardeth evil for good,
evil shall not depart form his house.
PROVERBS 17:13

S arah had tried everything she knew. She had been kind, she
had gone out of her way to be friendly, she had offered
Anne rides home, she had bent over backwards to help Anne
out, and she still was rotten to her. Sarah couldn't understand
why anybody would want to be so mean. Sarah's best friend
had told her that Anne was spreading terrible rumors about
her. This very night Sarah had tried to be friendly, and Anne
had called her names. Some of Sarah's friends said that Anne
was just jealous of her, but still, that didn't give her the right
to be so nasty.

It is hard to understand why people have to be so unkind.
We can try everything we know to be nice, and still there are
some who will not respond in kind. Those people are to be
pitied, for they will never know happiness or peace. There is
something that causes them to be terribly unhappy, and they
vent their sadness on those around them. Christ enables us to
return good for good, and even good for evil, but He never
likes to see us return evil for good. Happy and content is the
person who spreads happiness, but sad will be the person who
spreads evil, for the wrong done will never be escaped.

*PRAYER: O Lord, make me a doer of good works, and help me to
avoid doing things that are wrong or hurtful. Help me to understand the people who do evil to me, and guide me to try to help them
whenever I can. Amen.*

My Brother, My Friend

A friend loveth at all times,
and a brother is born for adversity.
PROVERBS 17:17

He couldn't believe it. He had worked for the same company for almost thirty years, and suddenly they pulled the rug out from under him. He had never known anything else. It seemed like all his hard work had been for nothing. He had been a good employee, and he had never made trouble. Now he felt ashamed for no good reason. He didn't know what he would do.

A knock at the door brought him out of his deep thought, and he got up to answer it. Outside, his brother waited for him. When he saw his brother standing there, tears came into his eyes. Whenever anything had ever gone wrong, his older brother had been there to make him feel better. Just seeing him stand there made him feel like there was nothing to worry about. No matter what happened, he knew he could always count on his brother. He had yet to face any bad situation without his brother to support him, and as long as he could lean on him, he knew everything would be just fine.

As children of God, we can be thankful that we have Christ to call a Brother. He will be with us in every situation, both good and bad. He will be our support and our counselor. He will listen without judging, and He will never leave us. He is as true as any brother could be, and we can count on Him to be there for us no matter what.

PRAYER: Thank You for being there when I need You. You are my strength and my shield. I am so grateful for Your love. Amen.

A MERRY HEART

A merry heart doeth good like a medicine:
but a broken spirit drieth the bones.
PROVERBS 17:22

Two men went into the hospital about the same time, having suffered similar heart attacks. One of the men grew depressed and irritable. He felt betrayed by his own body and saw his affliction as a sign of weakness. His attitude was sour, and he cursed his fate. The other man took it in stride. He kidded with everyone who came to visit him, and he laughed long and hard. He refused to be brought down by his plight. Instead, he occupied his time cheering up other patients and chatting with the staff. The first man grew weak and frail. The other man left the hospital in good health and resumed his old life quickly.

The way we face life has a lot to do with how good we will feel about it. If we are negative, then life will be a burden, but if we are positive, life will seem like the greatest gift we've ever known. Happiness is contagious. When we are happy, it spreads. However, sadness is contagious, too, and when we are gloomy, we spread a gray cloud over all the people we meet. A positive spirit is like a powerful medicine. It has a great deal of power to heal. It is so much better to face life with joy than to let life get you down. The person who feels that life is bad will wither and fail. God gave us life to enjoy, and He blesses us when we embrace it with happiness and contentment.

PRAYER: Fill my heart with joy that never ends. Let it overflow from my life to touch the lives of those around me. Make me a source of happiness for everyone I meet. Grace my countenance with a smile, bathed in the light of Your love. Amen.

BETTER TO REMAIN SILENT

Even a fool, when he holdeth his peace,
is counted wise:
and he that shutteth his lips is
esteemed a man of understanding.
PROVERBS 17:28

I t took every ounce of courage he had to say anything. He had always been shy, and he was terribly afraid of being made fun of. He knew that if he ever opened his mouth, he would say the wrong thing and be ridiculed. He had been that way all his life. People probably thought he didn't know anything, and that wasn't far from the truth. He wasn't overly bright, and that just added to his fear. It came as quite a shock to him, then, when one of the girls in his class came to him for help with her assignments. She told him that she had always thought that he was smart because he wasn't always talking and trying to impress everyone. What he feared most was that his silence would be taken as ignorance, while instead, it was being perceived as maturity and intelligence.

We don't have to be brilliant, but it is important that we learn to keep our mouths shut when the situation warrants it. No one likes a know-it-all, and it is much better to say too little than to always say too much. The wise person doesn't always have to be talking. Rather than awkwardness, they find comfort in silence. A fool speaks to cover silence and ends up saying silly and senseless things. The saying goes, "Silence is golden," and in many cases a truer word was never spoken.

PRAYER: I think that I have so much that is worth saying. Help me to remember that I learn more when I listen than when I speak. Help me to hold my peace and to give others time to share their thoughts and feelings. Amen.

THE PERSON OF THE WICKED

It is not good to accept the person of the wicked,
to overthrow the righteous in judgment.
PROVERBS 18:5

A landlord allowed a woman to take a room, knowing that she was a prostitute. He told her that he wasn't concerned with what she did, so long as she kept her business away from his property. He found out that she had begun to bring her customers to her room at night, and he went to have a talk with her. She defended her right to have anyone she wanted come to her room since she paid a good rent. He replied, "Look, I never passed judgment on you as a person, but I don't like what you do. You are always welcome on my property, but I don't have to allow you to do anything you please. It's nothing personal, it's just the way it is."

God feels much the same way. God loves every person completely. It is what we often do that God does not like. God wants no one to suffer or be punished, but there are certain things we do that He will not tolerate. God welcomes us into His house. If we want to dwell there, we must follow His rules and not try to make rules of our own. There is nothing any of us can ever do to make God stop loving us, but there are many things we can do which will cause Him to turn us away from heaven's gate.

PRAYER: Lord, make my behavior good and acceptable. Help me to see the errors in my thinking and acting. Lead me away from the things that offend You, and bring me to an understanding of behavior that will make me fit for heaven. Amen.

Pride and Destruction

Before destruction the heart of man is haughty,
and before honour is humility.

Proverbs 18:12

The opposing team came strutting out onto the court in brand new matching uniforms. The girls warmed up, and they acted cocky. They had been champions two years running, and you could tell that they thought they would have no trouble with the rag-tag band that was there to face them. The other girls looked a little lost on the volleyball court, and they wore whatever shorts and T-shirts they could throw together. The other team was intimidating just by their appearance, never mind their attitudes.

The games were close, but when the smoke cleared, David had once again knocked off Goliath. The former champs were not quite so haughty now. They looked down at their feet and offered insincere and unconvincing congratulations. Their spirit broken, they headed out of the gymnasium, while the giant-killers reveled in their victory.

Sinners kid themselves into believing that they are above the silly faith of Christians. They think that they are too good, too smart for God. When they find out they are wrong, they act as if they had never been told. Humility is a wonderful virtue. It assures the person that he can never be knocked down, because he was never too high in the first place. God blesses the person who realizes he is no better than anyone else.

PRAYER: You have created so many different kinds of people, dear Lord. Help me to love them all equally, never thinking that I am better than any of them. Grant that I might see Your image in every human being. Amen.

GIFT GIVING

A man's gift maketh room for him,
and bringeth him before great men.
PROVERBS 18:16

He had worked for this interview for months. He was about to interview one of the most popular actresses of all time, and he was very nervous. He knew little about her, really, except that she loved animals. He had picked up a stuffed dog on the way up to her apartment, just as a token of esteem, hoping that it would break the ice. She received it warmly, and he felt that he had made exactly the right move. She was truly appreciative of the small gift, and it made the atmosphere so much more comfortable for the interview. Afterwards, the reporter became great friends with the actress, and he frequently dropped in with more "pets" to add to her collection.

Gifts given from a pure heart are a real blessing. They let another person know that you care, and they pave the way for a deeper relationship. Often a well-timed gift can heal a wound or cement a relationship. It blesses both gift and giver, and it spreads a feeling that God loves. Giving is a powerful way to show what kind of person you are. Gifts freely given build bridges that last a lifetime. Nothing is finer than a gift given in love, as is evidenced by the divine gift of God's only Son, Jesus Christ our Lord.

PRAYER: Make me a giver, Lord. A giver of time, of talent, of love, of commitment, of peace, of gifts, of all the things that make life worth living. Help me to reflect Your giving spirit in every way possible. Amen.

THE POWER OF THE TONGUE

Death and life are in the power of the tongue:
and they that love it shall eat the fruit thereof.
PROVERBS 18:21

Pilate looked out over the crowds of people. So, it had come to this. People who usually had no use for him were now coming to him, looking for him to pass judgment on one of their own. It was exhilarating to have such power. With a word, he could bestow life or death. The Nazarene seemed totally unimpressed by his power, but the crowd knew better. They knew that his word was law! No matter how many times he was called upon to pronounce sentence, he still grew tense with excitement. This was power, and he loved it.

There is power in our words. Our tongues are like two-edged swords. They can protect and defend or they can cut down and destroy. We are in control of them. Sadly, many people act as if it was the other way around, that their tongues controlled their minds. As Christians, it is vital that we learn to control our tongues. James compares the tongue to a rudder. When a rudder is left untended, the ship flounders. Likewise, when our tongues move uncontrolled, the result is disaster. A wise person keeps a firm control over his or her words. Only words of life and light should be spoken, and with God's help, we can hope to always have such graceful speech.

PRAYER: O Lord, take control of the rudder and steer this humble vessel. Use the words of my mouth to minister to the needs of others. Let the will of my heart always precede the words of my mouth. Amen.

A FRIEND AT ALL TIMES

A man that hath friends must shew himself friendly:
and there is a friend that sticketh closer than a brother.
PROVERBS 18:24

A man moved into an apartment and held an open house in order to meet new people. Many people showed up, and they seemed to enjoy themselves enormously. He invited them to come back and frequently held parties that were the hit of the apartment complex. When he lost his job and the funds became scarce, he cut back on his entertaining. Many of his "new friends" stopped coming around. A few stuck with him, though, and they kept coming back regardless of what he had to offer them. They were most concerned with how he was doing. The others were merely concerned with what they could get from him.

Fair-weather friends are easy to come by. The real friend, one who will stand by you no matter what, is rare. It is devastating to think that we have good friends, just to find out that they could care less about us when we hit hard times. We need to have friends we know will stick with us in bad times as well as good. God is one such friend.

No matter what happens, God will be there when we need Him. He will never turn us away, and He loves it when we come to Him with our problems. There is no better friend that we can ever hope to have than God Himself. His love never fails.

PRAYER: Teach me what being a friend is all about, Lord. Let me see how You intended friends to act by being my friend. Make me ever to do for others what You do for me. Help me always to deal with people in love. Amen.

THE POOR AND THE RICH

Wealth maketh many friends;
but the poor is separated from his neighbour.
PROVERBS 19:4

It was hard. All through college they had been the best of friends. They had gone everywhere together and had done everything together. They had been inseparable. Since they had left college, though, things had changed. Her friend had married into money and taken a high-paying job herself. Meanwhile, she was working with poor families, and her salary was barely enough to feed her and pay the rent. Her friend didn't seem to have any time for her anymore. They had so little in common. Really, the only thing that had changed was their financial status, but that was enough to drive a wedge between them. Her best friend acted like she wasn't good enough anymore.

Money can change many things. It can cause us to act strangely, and it can turn our priorities upside down. The interests of the wealthy are usually not the interests of the poor. The poor cannot hope to reach up to the level of the rich, but those with money have a great opportunity to reach out to the poor. God calls us to give what we can to ease the burden of those who are less fortunate. Money should never close us off from anyone else, but it should ever open new doors for us to enter into God's ministry.

PRAYER: Lord, all that I have has come from You, and to You I commit it. Let me use my wealth to build bridges, rather than to dig chasms. Help me to befriend others not on the basis of economics, but on their worth as children of Yours. Amen.

KEEPING SIN IN THE PAST

The discretion of a man deferreth his anger;
and it is his glory to pass over a transgression.
PROVERBS 19:11

This was the third home she had been placed in, but it was by far the best. The first place she went, they tried to lock her in her room after dark. They punished her severely and even hit her. She had run away so many times that they put her back in the orphanage. The second home was like a hurricane. Everybody was fighting all the time. In tears, she had called the director of the home for girls, and they had come to get her. This new place was different, though. The people acted like they cared. The fact that she had run away so much, and that she had been sent to reformatory two times, didn't seem to make a difference to her new folks. They acted like they trusted her, and when she had asked them why, they had told her that all the other stuff was in the past. They would trust her until she gave them reason not to. She decided right then and there that she was going to try never to give them any reason.

It is so important for us to forgive people their past sins. When we mistrust someone because of his past, we apply a stigma to him that he fights all of his life. It is better to learn to forgive and to keep forgiving, so that the person can know that there is no judgment that will come from us. Judgment will come from the Lord. What should come from us is open and honest love and the gift of a second chance.

PRAYER: Lord, let me forgive those whom I meet, and grant that I might learn to forgive others as You have forgiven me. Amen.

IMPORTANT ACTIONS

A foolish son is the calamity of his father:
and the contentions of a wife are a continual dropping.
PROVERBS 19:13

He had just about had enough. It was bad enough that his son had been expelled from school for fighting. . .the third time, and that his wife kept defending their son, but then for them to get into a fight over the whole affair in public, it was just too much. All of his friends knew of the problems he had. They all knew that his son was no student and that he carried a chip on his shoulder continually. They also knew that his wife argued with him all the time. He couldn't stand all the pitying stares and the comments made supposedly behind his back. It hurt him deeply, and he felt helpless to do anything to change it.

It would be wonderful if all of our actions brought honor to our families. Unfortunately, that's an unrealistic hope. No one is perfect. We have to accept each other, flaws and all. Still, we should try to do everything we can to make our families proud of us. We should especially do everything in our power to make our heavenly Father proud of us. Christians are to be examples for others to follow, and when we dishonor God we do a very serious thing. Through our actions, we discredit the power of God to make us new people. Our foolishness causes calamity, and our resistance to His will makes other people doubt the power of our faith.

PRAYER: Lord, guide the steps of my feet. Help me to remember that the eyes of other people are on me, seeing the difference You have made in my life. When I dishonor You, I dishonor the entire faith. Forgive me. Amen.

GIVE TO THE FATHER

He that hath pity upon the poor lendeth unto the LORD;
and that which he hath given will he pay him again.
PROVERBS 19:17

A poor woman came to a rich young ruler and asked him for a few coins. The ruler turned her away, telling her to work for her food. A sick man came asking help, and he, too, was turned away. A friend who had come on hard times stopped and asked for assistance, but the young ruler told him to work for his wage. Then the Lord came to him, asking for a small loan. The rich young man said, "Lord, all that I have is Yours. Take what You will, and more." The Lord took from the ruler and gave to the woman, and to the man, and to that friend. He said to the ruler, "I come to you in many forms. When you give to any of these, then you give also to Me. Hold back nothing from those who ask, and your reward will be great in heaven."

It is hard to see sometimes, but when we give to a child of God, we give also to the Father. God loves to see us care for one another, and He abhors it when we turn away from others in need. The wise man or woman shares all he or she has, and asks nothing in return. God showed us this way when He gave His Son to be our Savior, requiring nothing more than that we believe. This is the seed of true believing, and it is within reach of all who will take it.

PRAYER: I sometimes turn my back to the poor. Help me to remember that I am really turning my back on You. Forgive me for my unkindness. Let me learn to be unselfish, and take from me what is really Yours, Father. Amen.

GETTING AHEAD

The desire of a man is his kindness:
and a poor man is better than a liar.
PROVERBS 19:22

Early in their marriage, she had loved her husband's gentle spirit and giving nature. He had spent time with the children, and he had loved the free time he could devote to his family. As the years passed, things changed. He devoted more and more of himself to his job. He became obsessed with getting ahead. The pressures he felt at work he brought home with him, and he vented his frustrations on his family. His once-gentle spirit had turned hard, and it appeared that he had forgotten how to give. She was very sad over the change and realized that part of it was her fault. She had grown accustomed to living well, and the only way their lifestyle could be maintained was through her husband's hard work. Deep inside, she wished that things would be different.

What we want inside will be apparent by the way we live our lives. Whatever we make our god, that we will pursue with all our hearts, minds, and spirits. If the Lord is the desire of our hearts, kindness and love will show forth; but if we pursue material gain, or fame, or prestige, then we will be devoid of kindness and warmth. It is much better to forsake all wealth in order to live purely and righteously. God smiles upon us when we remain true to His ways. When we live a life of kindness and caring, He rejoices.

PRAYER: Help me not to be swept up in the ways of the world. They lead down a false path to a poor reward. The path to heaven is a true path, and the reward is greater than anything this world has to offer. Amen.

STRONG DRINK

Wine is a mocker, strong drink is raging:
and whosoever is deceived thereby is not wise.

PROVERBS 20:1

It always started the same way. A voice in his head said, "One more won't hurt anything." But one more turned into five, and before he knew it, he was over the edge. This time it had caused him to miss work. Before, it had made him wreck his car. Once, it had put him in the hospital. Where was it going to end? He refused to believe he was an alcoholic. He only drank once every few months or so, but when he did, the results were disastrous. He was a moderately intelligent young man, but when he was drinking, all reason flew out the window.

God disapproves anytime we become prisoner to some substance. If we find that we cannot live without something, or that we cannot control our behavior, then that thing must be removed from our lives. There are no two ways about it. Christians are to be disciplined people, and it is vital that we learn to control our actions and our thoughts. Strong drink removes the ability to do that. Christians are constantly being examples of the truth of Christ. If we are controlled by other things, then we dishonor God. We must rise above the things that try to trap us, to show the liberating power of Christ in our lives. If we will ask Him, He will be faithful to give us the strength we need to kick any bad habit.

PRAYER: If there is anything in my life which You are ashamed of, Father, please help me to destroy it completely. I want to be a fine example of Your love and power. Make me over to be as good a person as I can be. Amen.

GET WHAT YOU GIVE

The sluggard will not plow by reason of the cold;
therefore shall he beg in harvest, and have nothing.
PROVERBS 20:4

There is a famous children's story about a little red hen that searched for other barnyard residents to help her bake bread. No matter where she went, all the other animals had some reason that they couldn't pitch in and help. Finally, she decided to bake the bread by herself, and soon the entire barnyard was filled with the enticing aroma of her coop-baked bread. When the other animals smelled the fine bread, they flocked around the chicken coop with their mouths watering. The hen peeked her head out and announced, "Everyone who helped make the bread gets a big slice with butter!" Whereupon, she proceeded to eat hers in front of a group of regretful loafers.

How sorry a day it will be when we are called to stand before the judgment throne of God if we have not chosen to follow His commandments. He has asked us to do what we know we should, and often we disobey, not through an evil spirit, but because of laziness. Just as the animals in the story, we can hope to receive no more than we were willing to give in this life. If we give nothing, then nothing will we receive. If we give much, our Father in heaven will heap an unending supply of good things upon us.

PRAYER: When a call comes for obedience or service, let me be the first to raise my hand to volunteer, O Lord. I do not want to be left outside in the last days. Welcome me into Your holy presence, Father. Amen.

PARTIALITY

Divers weights, and divers measures,
both of them are alike abomination to the LORD.
PROVERBS 20:10

She stormed into the classroom with her paper clenched in her fist. She marched up to the professor's desk and tossed her paper in front of him. A "C+" was scrawled across the head of the paper.

"Why was I given this grade? This is a good paper."

"Good for anybody else maybe, but not for you. You put forth average effort, and you got an average grade."

"That's not fair. My paper is better than most in the class, but a lot of people got A's."

"Look, I can give you any grade I please. I think you can do better, so I gave you a C+. That's it!"

"I'll fight it. It's not fair for you to judge some people one way and other people differently."

It is frustrating to feel like we are being taken advantage of. When we deal with other people, we like to think that we will be treated fairly. By the same token, we should be very careful in our dealings with other people to be sure that we always treat them fairly. God looks kindly on His children who deal with equality and fairness. Partiality is an abomination in the sight of God. We must always strive to do what we know is right.

PRAYER: Lord, let me look upon every person I meet as an equal. Help me to remember to treat them as I would like to have them treat me. Guard that I do nothing to offend or cause suffering. Amen.

OUR GREAT CREATOR

The hearing ear, and the seeing eye,
the LORD hath made even both of them.

PROVERBS 20:12

He stood looking on in awe. His son, his firstborn, was coming into the world, and he was a part of it. He stood by his wife's head, and together they shared the wonder of the experience. He had often doubted whether God existed, but now all of his doubts were gone. He looked on at the perfect little creation. Each finger and toe was a testament to God's loving existence. The miracle of life was overwhelming. It was inconceivable that something like this could happen by chance. Only a master artist of incomprehensible power and glory could come up with something so fine as human life.

When we look at God's creation, it is difficult to question anything about Him. There is so much to wonder at in the world. As we learn more and more, it should not make us skeptical of God. Quite the contrary, it should convince us that there is a grand author of all creation and that His power is far beyond our wildest imaginations. Only a foolish person would deny God's existence in the face of such remarkable evidence. To see God, all we must do is open our eyes and look around. His signature is on each one of His creations. He is right there for the person who has eyes to see and ears to hear. God is all around us.

PRAYER: O Lord, You are indeed everywhere. I look to the sky, and Your beauty and wonder meet my eye. I look around, and I see You in the faces of those I meet. I look inward, and thankfully, I see You in my heart. Amen.

No Harmless Gossip

He that goeth about as a talebearer revealeth secrets:
therefore meddle not with him that flattereth with his lips.
PROVERBS 20:19

A man was seen coming and going from a married woman's house. Her neighbor watched with fascination and concocted elaborate tales, which she shared with her friends as truth. There was no evidence any more incriminating than the fact that the young man came regularly, but the rumor was that the woman was having an affair. The "news" spread like wildfire, and wind of it eventually got back to the woman's husband. He confronted her in anger and hurt. The woman defended herself well. The young man she was seeing was her own brother, who came to the house to study between his classes. The senseless words of a gossip caused unnecessary pain to other people and planted a seed of doubt, which caused great trouble.

There is no such thing as harmless gossip. Gossip is wrong. It is talking negatively about someone who has no chance to defend himself. It is usually based on half-truths and sparse information. It isn't done to build someone up. It is done only to tear someone up. When we tell false stories about another person, we are stealing from him in the worst way. We take away dignity and honor, and we throw dirt on his reputation. It is an evil that God despises because of its basic cruelty. Lovers of the Lord are lovers of all His children. Therefore, we should speak of our sisters and brothers only as we would speak of the Lord Himself.

PRAYER: May my words be ever praiseworthy. Let no foulness or gossip pass from my lips, O Lord. Amen.

WISDOM OF THE AGED

The glory of young men is their strength:
and the beauty of old men is the gray head.
PROVERBS 20:29

A famous ball player reflected over a highly successful career. He had been a feared hitter, and no one had challenged his throwing arm from the field. He was well muscled and a fine athlete. He quit playing while he was still doing well, and it was a decision he felt good about the rest of his life. When he got old, he still had fine memories of his glory days, but that wasn't all he had. He had seen too many players who lived in their own pasts, and that was sad. He had used his time well, had made good investments, developed other interests, and he enjoyed a full and active life as a senior citizen. His strength had faded, his athletic days were behind him, but he had his mind, and no one could take that away from him.

Often we judge younger men by their physical abilities, while we judge older men by their wisdom. Age brings with it certain limitations, but it also gives certain strengths. Experience gives us a perspective on life that we can obtain no other way than by growing older. The aged in our world have a wonderful legacy to offer us in the form of their experiences and observations. They have walked a road that we are only beginning. Through their words we may come to know the traps that lie along the way, and they can help us over them, if we will only let them.

PRAYER: Lord, let me respect those who have lived longer than I have. Open my heart to their instruction, and let me revere them the same way that I revere You. Amen.

WHAT'S YOUR MOTIVATION?

Every way of a man is right in his own eyes:
but the LORD pondereth the hearts.
PROVERBS 21:2

Timidly, the man walked up to the pearly gates and cleared his throat. St. Peter peered at him from a high stool. Without a word, he pointed the man through a huge door, and inside was a throne. The man walked to the throne and said, "I'm ready for heaven, sir."

"What makes you think so?" a voice asked.

"Well, sir, I gave to the poor, I went to church, I never cheated on my wife, I didn't drink, and I prayed twice a day."

"You mean, you got tax deductions, you wanted people to think highly of you, you were afraid you'd get caught, you were allergic to alcohol, and you said grace before meals, don't you?"

"I was hoping you wouldn't know the difference," said the man.

Not only are our actions important, but our reasons for them are important, too. God sees us not as we appear to be, but as we really are. He knows every motivation for every move we make. We can't kid God, and we shouldn't try to. We may think we are doing all right if we do the things God asks, but more importantly, we need to do what He asks for the right reasons.

PRAYER: Eternal God, search the depths of my heart to see if I am doing all I can for the right reasons. Lead me to new ways of serving You. Help me to see what is lacking in my life, and support me as I try to change. Amen.

HEAR THE CRY

Whoso stoppeth his ears at the cry of the poor,
he also shall cry himself, but shall not be heard.
PROVERBS 21:13

Will you please turn that off? I can't stand seeing those little babies with their stomachs all stuck out and flies all over their faces. It makes me sick. I don't want to have to look at that junk and listen to those whining people beg me for money. It's all they do. I get tired of everyone trying to spend my money for me."

How different might that person sound if he were on the other end? One of the easiest things we can do is to take a moment to put ourselves in someone else's shoes. Whenever we see someone suffer, our hearts should go out to him. We should not just see a child in pain, but we should see Christ in pain. Our Lord Jesus Christ is a part of all creation. When we see people starve, we must remember His words, "Inasmuch as ye did it not [offer aid] to one of the least of these, ye did it not to me" (Matthew 25:44). We have been called to love each other as if we were loving God. To do less is to ignore the command of God and to stray into sin. We are the keepers of our brothers and sisters. If we ignore the pleas of those in need right now, then one day we will have to face the sad reality that our Father in heaven will not hear our own cry when we cry to Him.

PRAYER: Break through the hardness that exists around my heart. Open my ears to the cries of the poor, and open my eyes to the plight of the needy. Remind me to put myself in their place, and let me act accordingly. Amen.

IN THE FAST LANE

He that loveth pleasure shall be a poor man:
he that loveth wine and oil shall not be rich.
PROVERBS 21:17

It was his first real job. He was making a good salary, and he could now afford to live in style. He decorated his apartment, threw fantastic parties, and stayed out all night on the weekends seeking new and different thrills. He moved into the fast lane and spent money as fast as he could earn it. He had never done so much in his life. He bought all the things he'd ever wanted and many things he'd never dreamed of. He traveled and bought expensive gifts for his friends. Everything was as good as it could possibly be. . .until he was fired.

He had never believed his party could come to an end, but his lifestyle intruded on his work, and it led to his firing. Now he had nothing. No savings, no support, and no way to pay bills. His dream-come-true turned into a nightmare. He felt sick.

When we live for fun and self-indulgence, we live for nothing lasting at all. Our lives need meaning. They need a foundation. They need God. If we devote ourselves to Him, then we don't have time for frivolous endeavors that cause us to be selfish and wasteful. God will help us to live wisely and prudently. He will help us to know what is right and what is wrong. He will be faithful to do all of this, if we will only consent to put our trust in Him.

PRAYER: I do want to put my faith in You, God. I know that on my own I will give in to temptations that are selfish and foolish. Protect me from myself, O Lord. Guide me in the path of what is right and good. Amen.

GOD'S ARMY

A wise man scaleth the city of the mighty,
and casteth down the strength of the confidence thereof.
PROVERBS 21:22

L ong ago, a society built for itself many weapons and a great
wall around their city to protect them. They formed a
massive army, and they moved out into the world with the
hope of conquering it. They fought with anyone who tried to
stop them, and their empire grew. They came to a people,
however, who did not arm themselves with any weapons, yet
they refused to yield to the powerful war culture. They claimed
that they were strong by their faith in God, and that He was
the only protection they needed. The army battled them and
scattered them into foreign lands. Time passed, and the war-
ring nation fell, leaving no remnant behind. The people of
God reunited, and they were strong.

The people of God have never been defeated. Great em-
pires and armies have come and gone, but none have lasted as
long as the people who follow God. All else is refuse in comparison with the Lord. Mighty cities will rise, but they will
crumble long before the Lord comes to reward His faithful
ones. No army comes close to the might of God, and the greatest empire is not bigger than a speck of love of God. His might
endures forever, and His love shines brighter than the sun. Our
hope should always be in the Lord, and in Him alone.

PRAYER: My hope and trust is in You, almighty God. Only You
are God. Nothing else even comes close. There is nothing so mighty,
nothing so good as You, O Lord. Be with me always. Amen.

THE PROBLEM OF PRIDE

*There is no wisdom nor understanding
nor counsel against the LORD.*
PROVERBS 21:30

Lucifer, the most perfect of all of God's creation, looked to place himself on the same level as God. He wanted to be worshipped for his perfection, and he conspired against God. He grew jealous of the Lord, and he began to work against Him. He led one-third of the angels in revolt against the Lord, and he and his followers were cast from heaven.

The sin of pride is a dangerous one. It makes us think we are better than we really are. It leads us to judge others, and it makes us resentful of what we are not given. We disregard God's commands, and we begin to think only of ourselves. We close off all that is right and good, and we make ourselves out to be our own gods. We worship ourselves in subtle ways, and we rebel against the Lord by denying His will. Just like Lucifer, when we come before God, He will cast us away from Him. There is no place for sin in heaven, and the sin of pride is one of the worst. Sin finds its seed in selfishness, the sister of pride. God knows what is going on inside our hearts and minds. He can see right through us. If we will put our trust in Him and keep Him always as our Lord, then He will guide us away from pride and into a respect for all His children.

PRAYER: All secrets are open to You, O Lord. You know our comings and goings, and no thought goes by You unnoticed. Forgive my thoughts of pride and arrogance and lead me to a life of humble obedience and worship. Amen.

Mr. B.

A good name is rather to be chosen than great riches,
and loving favour rather than silver and gold.
The rich and poor meet together:
the LORD is that maker of them all.
PROVERBS 22:1–2

E veryone loved Mr. B. He was a friendly old man who loved
to play with children. Rumor had it that he was a brilliant
man who could have done anything he wanted, but one day
he walked out on his high-paying job, and he never returned.
Instead, he stayed home, began playing with the neighborhood children, and that had been how he'd spent his days ever
since. If a child was sick, he was right there to visit him. If a
child was hurt, he was the first to offer aid. If the familiar
ringing of the ice cream truck sounded in the distance, Mr. B.
was the first in line, ready to treat the neighborhood children,
no matter how many of them there were. His only purpose in
life seemed to be to spread joy to the children he met. He
never had a cross word, and he let them know that he loved
each and every one of them. He was a legend, and no one
who knew Mr. B. ever had anything bad to say about him.

When we give of ourselves, we find out what it really means
to be rich. Life takes on new meaning, and we are filled with a
feeling beyond description. God put us all here, and it is wonderful when we work together to make this life a joy. People
who live to love others are a blessing to the Lord. In those people, we can understand what it truly means to be happy.

PRAYER: Teach me what it means to be happy, Father. You are the
source of all that is good and right. Let me dwell within Your love,
and let me be a channel for Your love in this world that needs it so
very much. Amen.

THE EASY WAY

Thorns and snares are in the way of the froward:
he that doth keep his soul shall be far from them.
PROVERBS 22:5

The path looked like it would take forever. The house was just over the ridge, but the path wound all the way around the other side of the hill. The climb looked easy enough to go straight across. They left the path and started up the incline. The growth was thick and the footing was treacherous. As they reached the top, the way was blocked by thorn bushes and stickers that were too dense to push through, but when they turned to leave, the soft earth shifted, and they pitched into the brambles. The more they struggled, the worse the thorns stabbed and cut. By the time they made it back to the house, they were cut, bleeding, and exhausted.

Sometimes the easy way is not so easy. When we look for shortcuts, we need to be aware of the dangers along the way. The path that is laid out before us is there for a reason. With our Christian pilgrimage, we can be sure that God knows the best way for us to go. If we will trust His guidance and help, then we can be sure that the path we are on is the right one. He will never lead us wrongly. The only time we get into trouble is when we go off on our own, exploring places to which God does not lead us. As long as we always know to return to His path, everything will be okay.

PRAYER: I am tempted to walk many roads, not just the one I am on. Many seem to lead to exciting places, and others look so much easier than the one I am on. Help me to know that You have brought me to the best place I could possibly be. Amen.

TWO KINDS OF GIVERS

He that hath a bountiful eye shall be blessed;
for he giveth of his bread to the poor.
PROVERBS 22:9

There was a great need for a soup kitchen. He had driven all over town and stopped to talk to people he knew were living on the street. He went out on the streets and found the people where they lived. He was overwhelmed by the number of people who were going hungry; he could only do so much. He began visiting area churches and charities to see what support he could drum up for the kitchen. With widespread support, he knew great things could be accomplished. The need was there. Now, all that was needed was the commitment from others to do something about it.

There are two kinds of givers. There are those who give when they are asked, and there are those who go out and find ways to give. When we give only when we are asked, there is a danger of falling into an attitude wherein we hope no one will ask, and we will not be called upon to give. When we open our eyes and search for ways to give, however, we will not have to look too far, and we will find a way that we can serve. God wants us to follow the example of Christ, Who went to where the people were. We can shield ourselves from the poor if we try hard enough, but when we are honest, we know that they are there. They are waiting for us, and God urges us to take our duty seriously and do something now.

PRAYER: Where there is need, that is where I want to be, O Lord. Help me to give not only when it is convenient. Help me to look for need that I might give all the time. Amen.

GOD LOVES THE AFFLICTED

Rob not the poor, because he is poor:
neither oppress the afflicted in the gate:
for the LORD will plead their cause,
and spoil the soul of those that spoiled them.
PROVERBS 22:22–23

A man walked by a newsstand and looked over the magazines. He selected a couple of titles and prepared to pay for them. When he pulled out his wallet, he realized that the proprietor was blind. He looked at the stack of magazines and papers and he selected a couple more. He then told the man that he had selected one, and that the price was $1.75. He paid the man with two one-dollar bills, grabbed the four magazines, and strode away whistling. He called back over his shoulder, "Keep the change," and continued on his way, happy at the deception he had just pulled off.

There are people who look for ways to take advantage of anyone and everyone they can. They take delight in kicking others when they are down. They are cunning, ruthless, and merciless. God will have nothing to do with anyone who lives by abusing the poor and helpless. God is on the side of the meek, and when they are attacked, God is attacked. The poor may not be able to defend themselves, but God certainly is. He will remember those who work to spoil the afflicted, and He in turn will spoil their souls. God is love, and those who live by hatred and evil will have no reward from Him.

PRAYER: You have blessed the meek and the poor and those who mourn. Let me be among Your blessed, Lord. I rejoice when Your will is done. Let me spread Your love wherever I roam. Amen.

ANCIENT LANDMARKS

Remove not the ancient landmark,
which thy fathers have set.
PROVERBS 22:28

When the neighbors decided to sell their land, they thought little of it. Now it was a major dispute. The neighbors were claiming that they had ownership of part of their land. It would have been a moot point twenty years before. His father had set large stone pillars on the property line, and a fence stretched from one to the other. They had marked the boundaries clearly and concisely, but they had been removed long ago, and now there was nothing to show where the line was. The property deeds had somehow been lost, and it looked like the court might find in favor of the neighbors.

Sometimes we devalue the things our parents have done. We assume they acted impetuously and without cause. We lose touch with their wisdom and their desires. We destroy their legacy to us, bit by bit. This is most true of the teachings they gave us when we were young. Parents do their best to bring up their children in the best way possible. They do what they can and hope that some of it sticks. Our heavenly Father does the same thing. God has given us a legacy that has stretched over thousands of years. The tales of the Bible should give us instruction on how we should live our lives and what we should avoid. Often we choose to ignore the instructions, thinking that they are outdated. God's truth never grows out of date, and His instruction is as a lamp unto our feet.

PRAYER: Lord God, forgive me when I think that I know more than those who have gone before me. Help me to see the wisdom of history, especially my personal history, that I might discern all the treasures that have been left for me. Amen.

WINGS OF RICHES

Labour not to be rich: cease from thine own wisdom.
Wilt thou set thine eyes upon that which is not?
for riches certainly make themselves wings;
they fly away as an eagle toward heaven.
PROVERBS 23:4–5

His entire life he had wanted to be rich. He saved every penny he made and invested wisely. With money came power, and he aimed to be one of the most powerful men around. Over time, he came to desire money with all his heart. His investments became more and more risky as he tried for fast profit. All his life he had seemed to have a Midas touch, but then it turned to brass. A series of ill-advised investments ate up his wealth. In panic, he tried to recover his losses; but in his haste, he lost the rest of what he had. He had given himself totally to making money, and after a long life, he had absolutely nothing to show for it.

It is better to give ourselves to something that cannot be taken away from us. Money is here and then gone, but faith in God endures forever. The treasure He gives us is eternal. Joy, peace, strength, love, and a thousand other precious gifts can be ours if we will pursue God with all our hearts, minds, and souls. He is the only one worthy of such devotion. Everything else is a deception. It may seem worthwhile, but in reality, it is without value. Give your heart to God, and He will reward you beyond your wildest dreams.

PRAYER: I am surrounded by temptations which are temporary. They seem permanent, but they are frauds. Only You last forever, and in Your love will I find true wealth. Fill me with a treasure which cannot diminish. Amen.

UNFADING TREASURE

Buy the truth, and sell it not; also wisdom,
and instruction, and understanding.

PROVERBS 23:23

It looked like a great deal. He had wanted a new camera for a long time, and when he saw the one he wanted to buy for three hundred dollars less than any other price he had found, he jumped at the chance. It had worked well for a couple of weeks, but then the shutter stuck. After that, the pictures were coming out foggy. The lens didn't seat properly on the face of the camera, and the film started jamming. It didn't take long to realize that he had been taken. The camera he bought was nothing but junk. He had paid a foolishly low price, and he had been made a fool of.

There are so many things in our lives which look good, but they are really inferior. Fame, wealth, prestige, looks, all seem like they are wonderful things to have, but they fade away and leave us with nothing. Truth, wisdom, and understanding are costly, but they are worth anything we have to give. They fill us with an inner treasure which does not fade. There is nothing greater for us to devote ourselves to. God will guide us to wisdom and understanding if we will ask Him to. He blesses anyone who sincerely tries to find truth. With God on our side, we can rest assured that we will attain our goals. Once attained, we will never let go of the riches we have been blessed with.

PRAYER: There is a lot in this world that has no value. Keep me from giving myself to those things. Make me desire truth, wisdom, instruction, and understanding. I love You, Father, and I want to do what is right. Bless my efforts. Amen.

LOVING FAMILIES

Through wisdom is a house builded;
and by understanding it is established:
And by knowledge shall the chambers be filled
with all precious and pleasant riches.
PROVERBS 24:3–4

S he loved visiting her friends. Their whole family was wonderful. It was a joy to enter a place where there was so
much love and affection. They spoke to one another with
respect, and they showed kindness beyond belief. Even when
the girls did something wrong, they were treated with love
and care. She wished she could live in a home like that, and
she swore that when she was a parent, she would try to be as
fain and loving as her friends' parents were.

Families should be havens of love and support. We should
learn what love is all about from our families. We should also
learn what it means to truly love others, whether they deserve
it all the time or not. Unconditional love means love which
doesn't ask anything in return. Christians are called upon to
love all people, regardless of whether they are worthy of it. This
is the love which God gives to each one of us, and it is a love
that He hopes we will use in our relationships here on earth. A
house which is built upon kindness and understanding is a for-
tress against all the evil in the world. A good home is a blessing
beyond words. Establish a home in true love, and its benefits
will last forever.

PRAYER: Teach me what it means to love unselfishly, dear God.
Help me to judge no one, and to love everyone that I can. Forgive
me when I am unloving, and fill me with Your spirit, that I might
grow in Your ways. Amen.

THE REHEARSAL

If thou faint in the day of adversity,
thy strength is small.
PROVERBS 24:10

They had rehearsed the play a hundred times. A month of hard work was quickly coming to its pay-off. The play opened to a packed house, and the actors and actresses waited anxiously for the curtain to rise. The lines had been memorized, the costumes fitted, the makeup put on and taken off repeatedly, the lights were in place, and the performers were in their places. The production went smoothly most of the way, but one actor completely forgot his lines. Instead of covering for himself, he froze. The other actors covered as well as they could, and the play finished without further incident. The actor was replaced after a few more bungled performances, and the play went on to receive rave reviews.

The Christian life is a preparation for the glory which is to come. We rehearse our parts every time we follow in the footsteps of Christ. It is important that we know our parts well before we go to the judgment seat of Christ. Those who know their parts well have nothing to fear. But if we freeze, and we are found lacking, then we will be unfit for the Kingdom. Good actors and actresses dedicate themselves totally to their craft. Christians must do the same. Our faith must completely guide our lives. If that is true, then we, too, will meet with rave reviews in the last days.

PRAYER: I want to be skilled in the ways of righteousness and light, almighty God. Help me to know how You would have me to walk. Help me to be faithful to practice my faith continually. Amen.

DEATH OF A SINNER

Rejoice not when thine enemy falleth,
and let not thine heart be glad when he stumbleth:
Lest the LORD see it, and it displease him,
and he turn away his wrath from him.
PROVERBS 24:17–18

A popular kind of movie these days has a rough and rugged cop or detective wage war on crime. The bad guys are doubly bad, and the good guys are cunning, smart, and powerful. They speak with their fists and their guns. The movie makers work hard to get the audience on the good guys' side, and there is great cheering and applause when the bad guys get their due in the end.

It's sad that we feel like that when the bad guys meet their end. God's people should feel bad when sinful people die in their sin. When any child of God dies, it is a tragedy, never a reason for celebration. God loves all His children, no matter what they do. He wants them to come back to Him, and when they die in their sin, it breaks His heart. As we learn to feel with the heart of Christ, and to think with the mind of Christ, then we also feel great sadness at the death of a sinner.

As long as we live, we should dedicate ourselves to sharing the truth of Christ. We may be responsible for leading people out of the darkness and danger of sin into the light and protection of God's love. God rejoices at our efforts to bring our brothers and sisters into His love. If we will do so, He will bless us richly.

PRAYER: I am sorry that I often feel good when I hear of evildoers who have met with their own destruction. Help me to learn to love the sinner while hating the sin. Let me feel and see and act as You would, Lord. Amen.

PIOUS GOSSIP

These things also belong to the wise.
It is not good to have respect of persons in judgment.
He that saith unto the wicked, Thou art righteous;
him shall the people curse, nations shall abhor him:
but to them that rebuke him shall be delight,
and a good blessing shall come upon them.
PROVERBS 24:23–25

There was a faithful church woman who was renowned as a gossip and a tale-teller. She would go to others to share with them "in Christian love." What she was really doing was talking about others behind their backs. She prayed for people by saying they were possessed by evil, when in fact their only sin was to disagree with her. Some perceived her to be holy, but most people knew of her terrible hypocrisy. Finally, they came to her and let her know that what she was doing was completely unchristian and destructive.

We have no right to judge anyone, and we should not use our piety to put others down. Our prayers should be prayers of love for God's guidance and protection, not for selfish and judgmental concerns. We accomplish nothing by talking ill of any other person, and we sin grievously when we try to mask it in Christian piety. We should try to help others understand God, but we must enter into that quest as equals. We need to make sure that our motives are always pure when we seek to help another person.

PRAYER: Lord, help me help others without feeling proud or vain. You have changed my life, and I am better off now than ever before, but do not let that change cause me to feel superior in any way to any of my brothers or sisters in Christ. Amen.

What's in Comes Out

I went by the field of the slothful,
and by the vineyard of the man void of understanding;
And, lo, it was all grown over with thorns,
and nettles had covered the face thereof,
and the stone wall thereof was broken down.
PROVERBS 24:30–31

Everyone remembered the property in its glory days. The house was enormous, and it was beautiful. The lawn had always been well groomed, and there was a magnificent garden in the back. Now it was a disgrace. The lawn looked like a field, the house was dirty, and mortar was crumbling from between the bricks. Vines covered the face of the building and the backyard looked like a garbage dump. The new owners were rarely home, and they did little to keep the property up. In the three years they had lived there, they had not mowed the yard once. The neighbors complained, but the residents said they had the right to live any way they chose.

Although it is wrong to judge a person based on appearance, often we can get an indication of what people are like on the inside by watching from the outside. If we live a holy life, it will be apparent in the way others see us. If we are slothful, others will be able to tell just by looking at us. Sometimes there are extenuating circumstances which cause even the most upright people to be negligent, but usually a person who is disciplined and committed to God will make every effort to put forth a good example.

PRAYER: Father, let what is in my heart be obvious to all who might look. Let my outside reflect the goodness which You have put inside. Amen.

THE POTTER

Take away the dross from the silver,
and there shall come forth a vessel for the finer.
PROVERBS 25:4

He worked the clay with skill, smoothing and turning it. It began as a lump, but in his hands, it took shape. He crafted it into a fine pitcher, but as he worked, he noticed that some of the clay was lumpy, so he started afresh. He reworked the clay, adding water and kneading it back and forth. He flipped the clay back onto the potter's wheel and began again. This time as he worked, he discovered a small stone in the clay, and once again, he started over. He worked the clay thoroughly, making sure that all of the impurities were out of it, and once satisfied, he crafted his earthen vase.

In the case of clay, or of silver, it cannot be used unless it is pure. If it is used in its imperfection, it will be flawed and worthless. We are like clay in God's hands when we give our lives back to Him. We ask Him to take us and shape us and to remove all our imperfections. Only by being perfected in His hands may we ever hope to have a place in heaven. God will not settle for less than what is perfect. In His hands we will be recreated, as God intends us to be. He will take away all that is bad or imperfect, and He will create from us a vessel acceptable and worthy to have a place in His kingdom.

PRAYER: I am filled with imperfections and flaws. Left as I am, I cannot hope to have a place with You, almighty God. Take me and start anew. Reshape me into the person You want me to be. Create in me a holy and good spirit, and bless me all of my days. Amen.

Snow at Harvest

As the cold of snow in the time of harvest,
so is a faithful messenger to them that send him:
for he refresheth the soul of his masters.

There was no doubt about it; harvest time was the hardest time of year. The planting and tilling and weeding were difficult, but harvest required every ounce of strength and stamina a soul could muster. When the days were cool, it made the job so much more pleasant, but when it was hot, there was no worse job on earth. The fields baked in the hot sun, and you baked also. Many a farmer came to his end out in the fields at harvest time when the sun was hot. This year was great. The snow was moving south from the hills, and the air off the plains was cold and brisk. Working in weather like this made you feel alive. It was refreshing and made you feel like you could work forever without stopping.

The breath of the Lord is like that. When we live without it, we are amazed at how hard this life is. We feel completely drained and exhausted by the simplest of tasks. When we have the Lord in our lives, however, He gives us strength and renews our stamina. With God all things are possible, and when His Spirit is in our hearts, we feel as if we can last forever without pausing. We are made conquerors with Christ, and nothing can defeat us.

PRAYER: Renew me, Father, in those times when I feel that I cannot go on. Forgive me when I try to live life all by myself, turning from Your loving care. Give me Your Spirit that I might rise above the struggles of this life and claim the victory won for me by Christ. Amen.

DON'T ADD VINEGAR

As he that taketh away a garment in cold weather,
and as vinegar upon nitre,
so is he that singeth songs to a heavy heart.
PROVERBS 25:20

A woman lay in her hospital bed, crying. The diagnosis had been cancer, and it was inoperable. While she was sobbing, a friend came in to see her. She asked the woman what was wrong, and the woman told her. Her friend patted her hand and said, "Where is your faith? Everything will work out just fine, as long as you have faith. God must have some reason for letting this happen, so just sit back and watch Him work."

The woman felt a strange anger in her heart. She knew her friend was trying to be helpful, but her words stung and were terribly unfair. She had plenty of faith. That had nothing to do with it. She had cancer, and that was something she wasn't prepared to deal with. Her friend acted like she hadn't even heard.

God never causes bad things to happen. He does indeed take bad things and turn them into good, but we have no way of knowing what He has in mind. When we try to comfort others, we need to connect with their pain and suffering. Offering them easy answers and platitudes does not help at all. We merely add to the person's suffering. We end up giving nothing of value, and, in fact, it is as if we pour vinegar into their wounds or take from them a cloak in the cold of winter. We do more harm than good.

PRAYER: Lord, let me listen to the cries of others and respond from my heart, where You are Lord and Master. Make me a compassionate, loving friend when others suffer. Amen.

CRUEL PRANKS

He that hath no rule over his own spirit
is like a city that is broken down, and without walls.
PROVERBS 25:28

The evening had begun with the usual Halloween pranks. Smoke bombs and toilet paper for trees, soap for windows, and an occasional water balloon for the unsuspecting passersby. Then the older boy from down the street had joined in. He had grown tired of the pranks and suggested they try some more exciting tricks. Under his guidance, the band of kids slashed some tires and broke glass in driveways. They poured oil on people's front steps and they threw rocks at windows. What had started as an evening of mischief turned to adolescent terrorism. The children went wild with their destruction, causing the residents to dread the idea of Halloweens yet to come.

Even the most innocent prank is still going to hurt someone. When we make another person a victim, we take from him his rights to security and comfort. When pranks get out of hand because we lack self-control, they can be dangerous and cruel. If we don't have any self-control, then we don't have the will to say "no" when we should. We need to pray to God for His strength and wisdom so that we resist the temptation to do the things we know we shouldn't. Discipline is an important part of the Christian life, and if that is what we lack, then we must seek it with all our hearts.

PRAYER: Help me to resist evil, O Lord. I know that I am sometimes weak, and I need Your strength to get me through. Help me to develop self-control and discipline in my life, Father. Amen.

DON'T JOIN THE FOOL

Answer not a fool according to his folly,
lest thou also be like unto him.

PROVERBS 26:4

It had gotten all over the school that Andrew's mother had gone to a mental institution. Most of the children were sympathetic, and they didn't tease him, but there were some who went out of their way to torment him. He tried to ignore their insults, but finally it got to be too much for him. Whenever one of the children would say something cruel, Andrew would strike back, saying terrible things in return. His anger overwhelmed him and he found himself getting into fights to defend his mother. Even the children who were sympathetic didn't want to be around him because of the anger he showed. He looked for weaknesses and skeletons in the closets of his classmates, and whenever he found out something that they would be ashamed of, he spread it around school.

Some people can be very cruel, but that is no reason for us to reply in kind. Jesus was tormented and ridiculed by many people in His lifetime, and He let the insult bounce right off. There was no way that Christ would ever have returned an unkindness. We are called to be loving, giving people, even to those who would try to hurt us. God blesses those who will remain loving in the face of cruelty, and His anger will be against those who do wrong.

PRAYER: Evil is contagious, O Lord. When one person does something cruel, and another person replies cruelly, then a cycle begins which can be broken only by love. Give me the love to heal anger and cruelty, Father. Amen.

TWISTED SCRIPTURE

The legs of the lame are not equal:
so is a parable in the mouth of fools.
PROVERBS 26:7

The discussion always came around to religion. She was a devout woman who read her Bible daily, prayed morning and evening, and went to church weekly. He, on the other hand, was neither a believer nor a nonbeliever; he just liked to argue. The problem was that he had read the Bible, and he knew it inside out. She would try to explain her beliefs to him, and he would tear them apart using Scripture as his support. It always made her angry to the point of tears. She knew he was twisting Scripture to make it say what he wanted it to say, but she didn't have the knowledge she needed to combat it. He took the Bible and made it into a joke.

When foolish people get ahold of the Bible, they can do some pretty terrible things with it. They twist its meaning, and they use it for selfish reasons. Nonbelievers love to take the Bible apart and quote it out of context. They like to misinterpret it in order to make believers appear foolish. How much more foolish they will look before the judgment seat of God when they are called upon to explain themselves. God gave us the Bible as a comfort and a support, not as a topic for debate. If we will spend time in Scripture, it will prove a faithful friend, and no one will be able to take its riches from us.

PRAYER: I fall into the trap of defending my faith, Father, when I have nothing to defend. Christ defended Himself with His resurrection, and He needs no further defense. Help me to remember not to argue my faith, but to live it. Amen.

Returning to Folly

As a dog returneth to his vomit,
so a fool returneth to his folly.
PROVERBS 26:11

All his friends thought that he was crazy. He loved to dodge cars as they sped along the highway. He would wait behind a bush until the car was too close to stop, then he would take off running across the road. The drivers would usually hit their brakes and come to a screeching halt, and to date, he had never even been scratched. After it was over, he would laugh and brag about it to all his friends. No matter how much they pleaded with him, he insisted on playing his stupid game. He called it bravery, but they thought he was a fool. One day he wouldn't be so lucky, and then who would he brag to?

God gave each of us a measure of common sense, and He expects us to use it. We have no right to do things that are a danger either to us or the people around us. God expects us to use the brains He has given us for constructive purposes. A dog vomits and then eats the vomit because of not knowing any better. We should have a bit more intelligence than the canine. When we do something that is foolish or wrong, we should know not to keep repeating it until disaster strikes. God blesses those who will use their talents and gifts for what is right and good, not what is foolish.

PRAYER: *I know that I do plenty of silly things, O Lord. Help me to stop being foolish, and empower me to use the mind and body that You have given me for good works. Let me see the errors I make, so that I do not repeat them. Amen.*

Mind Your Own Business

He that passeth by,
and meddleth with strife belonging not to him,
is like one that taketh a dog by the ears.
PROVERBS 26:17

A man was passing by a store when he saw two other men fighting. At first it was just a quarrel, but as tempers flared, both men took to scuffling. Blows were exchanged, and the man threw himself into the middle, trying to break the combatants apart. A knife was drawn, and in the confusion, the innocent man was stabbed. He fell to the ground, and the other two men took flight.

Our inclinations might be to intervene in matters that we feel are wrong. In many cases, we can be of some service, but often we should mind our own business. We can get ourselves into trouble that is unnecessary. It is as foolish to enter into a fight that is beyond our control as it is to try to take hold of a rabid dog. The only result will be that we will come out losers.

God gives each person freedom to choose. Some people will abuse that freedom, and they will try to hurt others with it. They will have to answer for that before God. Each of us needs to ask what Christ would do in a similar situation. Christ knew when to leave well enough alone. He knew when to enter in and when to stay back. God wants us to be useful, but He wants us to use our reason before we leap in where angels would fear to tread.

PRAYER: Lord, open my eyes. I so often act without reason and without foresight. Help me to know when to act and when to wait. Amen.

HONEST LIVES

Whoso diggeth a pit shall fall therein:
and he that rolleth a stone, it will return upon him.
A lying tongue hateth those that are afflicted by it;
and a flattering mouth worketh ruin.
PROVERBS 26:27–28

She couldn't believe what was happening. She had accepted a date for Friday night with a man she was seeing off and on. Then, out of the blue, her boss had asked her out. She had dreamed of that happening ever since she got the job. She reluctantly called her date for the evening and told him that she had become very ill and that she wouldn't be able to go out. Then she prepared herself for her evening with her boss. It was a wonderful evening, and she kept trying to tell herself that what she had done was perfectly fine. They were riding the elevator up to her floor, and she was anticipating a nice ending to the evening in her apartment. When the elevator doors opened, her sometimes-boyfriend was sitting across from it. He had come to spend the evening with her because he felt sorry for her. Suddenly, the guilt of what she had done swept over her, and she began to cry.

Each time we tell a lie, we set a trap. Someone might find out. Most lies have the potential of hurting someone. We do not have the right to do anyone harm. God watches each of us to see whether we will commit ourselves to living lives of truth or not. When we choose correctly, He rejoices and blesses us richly.

PRAYER: I want to be an honest person, showing my love and respect for other people by my honesty. Help me to destroy that part of me that is prone to lie and deceive. Give me a portion of Your truth by which I might live. Amen.

HUMILITY

Let another man praise thee,
and not thine own mouth;
a stranger, and not thine own lips.
PROVERBS 27:2

The quarterback stood before the reporters, giving them his views of the upcoming game.

"I really don't think we have much to worry about. We have prepared for this game, we have a stronger defense, a stronger offense, and I am definitely a better quarterback than my opponent. My statistics speak for themselves. I've out-performed him in every category. He's good, but I'm better."

The interview ended, the game was played, and it was an upset. The opposing quarterback threw rings around his adversary, and the words that bragging quarterback had uttered hours before were spread far and wide through all the major news services.

When we compliment ourselves, we open ourselves to disaster. Pride comes before a fall, the saying goes, and it is true. We cannot fall if we never set ourselves up above everyone else. When we do something well, we should content ourselves with the appreciation of others and not fall into the trap of conceit and arrogance. God loves humility, and His blessing is upon all who will think more highly of others than they think of themselves. Our praise should be for God and for others, but never for ourselves.

PRAYER: Lord, teach me humility and grace. I too often think that no one else can do things as well as I do. I get a wrong picture of my importance. Put my life into perspective, that I might live as I ought to. Amen.

THE KISS

Faithful are the wounds of a friend;
but the kisses of an enemy are deceitful.
PROVERBS 27:6

Jesus waited in the garden. His disciples had dozed off, and He was left alone to speak with God. He prayed hard and long, and when He finished, He looked up to see the approaching torches of soldiers and magistrates. He awakened His disciples, and to their amazement, one of their own was leading the aggressors. Judas looked upon Christ, and he felt icy. He moved forward to embrace the Lord, then kissed Him on the cheek, as if to say good-bye and that he was sorry. Jesus pulled back and said through pain and anguish, "A kiss? You come and you betray me with a kiss?"

Have you ever thought how painful that action was to Christ? An act usually associated with love was used to signal destruction. Someone that Christ had trusted and befriended paid Him back by turning Him over to the authorities, and he did it with a kiss.

There are times when a friend will strike us in order to wake us up to danger, or to bring us back to reality. Those blows are a blessing. But when someone hurts us under the pretense of love, that is the worst kind of pain. God wants us to deal with each other honestly. We cannot have things both ways. If we are not for God, we are against Him, and we should never compound our crime with hypocrisy.

PRAYER: Each time I sin, Father, I betray You with a kiss. I claim to love You, but then I do the things which I know You hate. Please forgive me, Lord. Help me to be better, I pray. Amen.

CONSIDERATION

He that blesseth his friend with a loud voice,
rising early in the morning,
it shall be counted a curse to him.
PROVERBS 27:14

It was not always easy being a night owl. Staying up late was only a pleasure when she was allowed to sleep late. Since they had moved to the new neighborhood she had met a few people, and they all arose around six A.M. That was fine if that's what they wanted to do. The problem was that they called her up after breakfast, which for them was seven o'clock. She knew that they were just trying to be friendly, but sometimes she wanted to scream at them. She had tried nicely to tell them that she liked sleeping in, but they still called by eight o'clock. She didn't know how long she would be able to tolerate their friendliness until it drove her completely crazy!

Consideration is an important Christian quality. If we love and respect other people, then we will want to know what is pleasing to them, and we will try to accommodate them. If we force ourselves on others, then we are being selfish. God does not want anyone to force their will on anyone else. Instead, He wants us to do for others everything in our power to make them comfortable and happy. To serve means to do what other people need and want. We do not get to set the rules, but we follow the rules of love set down by God.

PRAYER: Lord, I sometimes think I know what is desired of me, but I don't always ask. Help me to be sensitive to the needs of others, that I might serve them and bring them joy and comfort. Amen.

TAKE RESPONSIBILITY

Be thou diligent to know the state of thy flocks,
and look well to thy herds.

PROVERBS 27:23

A man was entrusted with a fine herd of cattle, and he was hired to transport them across the plains. Each morning he gathered the riders together and they began the long day's ride. Each night they settled in and left no one to guard the herd. By the time they arrived at their destination, they found that they were missing almost a hundred head. The owner of the herd refused to pay the man because he had been so careless in his duty.

When we take on a responsibility, we are obligated to do the very best we can. We have no right to take liberties with possessions that do not belong to us. When someone is counting on us, we owe it to that person to give everything we can to serve him. God wants us to serve others with as much devotion as we serve Him. When we give anything less than our best, we cheat ourselves, we cheat the people we serve, and most importantly, we cheat God. If we have an obligation, we must fulfill it or else we become liars and sluggards. God blesses those who will always give everything they have serving others. He is eager to bless His children, and He gives great reward to those who will be obedient.

PRAYER: Lord, teach me how You want me to live. Whenever I can, help me to serve others. Let me be steadfast and trustworthy, and let my integrity be a sign that You have made me new, in Your image. Amen.

DISASTROUS FLOODS

*A poor man that oppresseth the poor
is like a sweeping rain which leaveth no food.*
PROVERBS 28:3

The crops were almost in ruin. If rains didn't come soon, the people in the village would face another year of starvation. The forecasts had been dismal for so long that the people could hardly believe it when rain was predicted. They waited in excited anticipation. The clouds began to form, the wind to blow, and the blessed moisture began to drop. But the storms kept building, and the winds increased. The water pounded the ground, and it beat upon the crops. The food supply which had so desperately needed water was completely wiped out by storms and flooding when the rains finally came. It had been like a cruel joke played upon the people.

We see the rich of this world oppressing the poor, and it seems almost natural, but when the poor do things to hurt each other, it is amazing. It is as if they forget their poverty themselves and inflict worse on their neighbors. It is senseless and cruel, and it strikes with the force of a terrible storm. It is hard to defend or deal with because it is so unexpected. We feel that the people most like us will relate to our plight and be sympathetic. Evil strikes in every place, though, and it is by God's grace that those who are faithful will at last be saved.

PRAYER: I do things that are cruel to the people I should be most kind to. Forgive me when I do such foolish and hateful things. Father, help me to be thankful for Your grace and love. Let my thanks be shown through my love for others. Amen.

SHADY DEALINGS

Better is the poor that walketh in his uprightness,
than he that is perverse in his ways, though he be rich.
PROVERBS 28:6

It was the offer of a lifetime. He had the chance to invest in a project that was sure to make money. His brother brought the proposal to him to let him in on it. He was tempted, but there was a drawback. The project entailed driving some people from their homes in order to get some building done. There were some shady dealings going on, and the people were being robbed by the company doing the building. None of the homeowners was even remotely aware of the value of their property. He thought long and hard about the offer, but he eventually decided against it. Anything that made him money at other people's expense wasn't worth the guilt. Better to stay poor and be able to look yourself in the eye in the mirror than to be rich and hate yourself for it.

Some things just aren't worth the compromise they entail. If we have to give up too much, then we find it harder and harder to live with ourselves. The poor person who feels good about himself is far richer than a wealthy person who lives with shame and guilt. God will bless the person who holds fast to values by granting peace and comfort.

PRAYER: Lord, I feel good that I have a chance to serve You. Help me never to compromise my values and beliefs. Let all of my actions reflect the love and devotion that I feel toward You. Amen.

WISDOM OR CRAFT?

The rich man is wise in his own conceit,
but the poor that hath understanding searcheth him out.
PROVERBS 28:11

He had built for himself an empire. He was a powerful man. He controlled the lives of thousands of people. He manipulated millions of dollars and literally had the power of life and death in his hands due to foreign investments. His home was a mansion, and he hadn't driven for himself since he got a chauffeur ten years earlier. He had everything, and he prided himself on the brains he had used to get where he was.

We sometimes confuse cunning and craftiness with wisdom. We think that the ability to out-think and out-maneuver other people makes us more intelligent. Intelligence has nothing to do with it. A truly intelligent person would know that you don't treat other people like pawns in a game. Wisdom would tell a person that money was not the path to happiness. Wisdom would tell even the richest and most powerful man that he did not get all his blessing on his own. God created this world, and everything in it belongs to Him. We possess it for a short time, but the Lord owns it forever. God gives us material wealth so that we can use it for the good of others. Abundance is for sharing, not for hoarding. The one who prides himself in the wisdom that brought him wealth has no real idea of what wisdom is.

PRAYER: Almighty God, You are the author of all creation and the owner of all that is. Help me to remember that without You I would have nothing. All good things come from You, and I am thankful. Amen.

RESPECT BUILT ON LOVE

As a roaring lion, and a ranging bear;
so is a wicked ruler over the poor people.
The prince that wanteth understanding is also a great oppressor:
but he that hateth covetousness shall prolong his days.

PROVERBS 28:15–16

The jungle was silent. The animals sensed the presence of their lord. A thundering roar cut loose and sent the animals scurrying for cover. No animal dared confront the lion who ruled over the jungle land. His presence commanded respect and worship. However, it was a respect built on fear, not on love. As long as the beast had ruled, he had never known love. His subjects bowed to him, and they ran in fear, but he had never known what it meant to be well thought of.

Our Lord is a Lord of both power and love. It is well to fear the Lord, for He alone holds the power of true life and death. But we cannot have a relationship with anyone based on fear. There must be love, and our God makes it easy to love Him. He has given us a wonderful gift by giving us life, and He has proven His love for us by sending His only Son, our Lord Jesus Christ, to take the punishment for our sins so that we might one day be reunited with Him. Only a loving God gives so much to His children. We can rejoice that we do not serve a tyrant or a hateful master, but we serve the source of all that is good and right. His goodness shall endure forever, and we will be a part of it.

PRAYER: Thank You for not controlling me or forcing me to love You. I could not worship a God Who made His children fear Him. Please help me to be the person You created me to be, so that I might return the love to You which You have given to me. Amen.

LESSONS IN WISDOM

He that rebuketh a man
afterward shall find more favour than he that
flattereth with the tongue.
PROVERBS 28:23

A gifted tennis player rose to the top of her team with ease. She was hailed as a potential star on the pro circuit. All of the publicity went to her head, and she began to believe all the hype. She got to the point where she thought she was too good to associate with her teammates. She basked in the glory of her success and grew conceited. As she prepared for semi-finals, she broke curfew, and the coach sat her down and refused to let her play. She raged and fumed at the treatment, but the coach said, "I don't care who you think you are. You play for my team, and so you follow my rules. I don't treat you any differently than any other of the girls. You need to learn really fast that being good at a sport doesn't make you a better person than everybody else. The quicker you learn that the better."

The girl never forgot the experience, and the words of her coach stuck with her and saved her from a lot of pain and frustration in the future.

True wisdom is a friend throughout our lives. The truth is often not pleasant to hear, but if we will accept it, it will help us through many situations. The flatterer gives nothing of lasting value. It is the person who is willing to offer rebukes as well as praise who will give the greatest gift.

PRAYER: The truth is hard to hear many times, but that doesn't mean I don't need it. Open my heart to the truth, and let me always be accepting of Your guidance. I count on You to help me through the tough times, and to share in my good times. Amen.

TEST THE ICE

He that trusteth in his own heart is a fool:
but whoso walketh wisely, he shall be delivered.
PROVERBS 28:26

It had been years since he had gone ice-skating. As he looked out across the frozen pond, he was overwhelmed by a wave of nostalgia. He tested the ice with a boot, then took a few more steps onto the pond. He remembered the warnings of his mother when he was young. She had always told his younger brother and him to be careful and to test the ice before they went out on it. He had always remembered the rule. Too bad his brother hadn't. His brother never listened to Mom and Dad. He acted like he knew what was best. One time they had gone out to skate, and his brother had just waltzed out onto the ice. It was too thin, and before anything could be done, his little brother had drowned.

When we think that we always know best, we open ourselves to disaster. Wisdom comes from learning to listen to the counsel of others. When we are mature, we realize that others offer warnings and advice to protect us, not control us. The wise listen to friends and elders, and are made stronger. The foolish decide that their wisdom is all they need, and so wander alone down the road to destruction.

PRAYER: Help me not to trust so much in my own wisdom, heavenly Father. Let me see that there are many things I have yet to learn. Give me patience and perseverance that I might come to know that which will save me from my own foolishness. Amen.

GIVERS OF JOY

When the righteous are in authority,
the people rejoice:
but when the wicked beareth rule,
the people mourn.
PROVERBS 29:2

I n a small New England town, a bank and a library prepared
for the holidays. The week before Christmas, the library
announced that there would be a party to celebrate a good year
and a Merry Christmas. The bank made no such announce-
ment. The president felt that a Christmas party was beneath
the dignity of a bank. He said that business would be carried
on as usual, and that was that. The people in the library felt
that Christmas had come early. They were appreciative of the
consideration, and the atmosphere was happy and festive. At
the bank, the people felt a sadness. The Christmas spirit had
been stifled, and the atmosphere was heavy and gray. It takes
very little to make people happy. A little giving goes a long
way. When we deny people even the smallest kindness, they
lose spirit, and there is no joy. People rejoice under kind leadership, but harsh and unthinking leadership gives rise only to
mourning. God loves a cheerful giver, and He doubly loves
givers of joy. If we will remember the great love that God has
shown us, it will be easy to show a little of that love to the people we deal with day in and day out.

PRAYER: Let me sow seeds of kindness, Lord, that people might
know of my great love for You. You have given so much, now help
me give a little. Being kind is not hard, and it costs so little. Help
me to give it freely and abundantly. Amen.

WHAT THE FATHER SAID

The bloodthirsty hate the upright:
but the just seek his soul.
PROVERBS 29:10

The headlines screamed of the atrocity. A young woman had been killed while she was home for the holidays. She had been assaulted and beaten and then killed. It was shocking any time it happened, but there was something that made it worse during the holidays.

The woman's family would remember this every year when the season rolled around, and it would place a cloud over the celebrations.

The killer was caught just before Christmas, and the parents of the girl wanted to see him. They went into a room where a guard brought in the accused. For a moment they sat looking at each other, then the father said, "I don't know why you killed our baby, and I don't really care. I want to hate you, but I can't. God gave His Son so that I might have life, and now I've given my daughter. I hope that her life makes a difference. We came to tell you that we're praying for you, and we hope you really repent of what you have done. We won't stop praying until you're dead or saved." With that, the couple left.

PRAYER: Your gift to me in the life of Your Son is greater than I can comprehend. I want to know that love in my life. Help me to pray for the evil people in this world, that they might know the truth and love that You freely give. Amen.

ALL MADE EQUAL

The poor and the deceitful man meet together:
the LORD lighteneth both their eyes.
PROVERBS 29:13

He hated having to walk to work. His office was in the center of a poor part of town. The beggars sat along both sides of the street, and he couldn't stand to smell their smell, to see their faces, or hear their pitiful begging. He hurried through the streets, and the question ran through his mind why God made him suffer like this. He wished the poor would go off and find some other street to haunt. It bothered him that he even had to share the sidewalk with some of these characters.

As he approached his office, he saw, from the corner of his eye, yet another group of poor people clustered outside a church. He walked past them, feeling outraged that they even littered the lawn of the church. He decided enough was enough. He turned to speak his piece to the group, but what he saw made him stop. His heart sank, and he felt a pang of guilt and shame in his stomach. The group on the lawn was the nativity scene. The poor were Mary, Joseph, and the Babe, and suddenly the evil of his thoughts was made clear to him.

God has made us all, and He has made us equal. If we reject poor people because they make us feel guilty or uncomfortable, then we must remember that we would reject Christ Himself, Who never made a claim to prominence or wealth.

PRAYER: Let me accept all people just as they are. Open my eyes so that I can see the Christ which exists in all of Your children. I love You, Lord; I want that love to grow as large and strong as is possible. Amen.

LISTENING TO LEARN

Seest thou a man that is hasty in his words?
there is more hope of a fool than of him.
PROVERBS 29:20

The rush was on. The woman stood bewildered in the department store. Her husband had asked especially for a certain razor, and she was determined that she would get it for him. She finally got a sales clerk to wait on her, and she told him what she wanted. He looked at the counter, and then went into a fast sales pitch for a razor that was on sale. Five times she repeated what she wanted, and five times he tried to sell her something else. In frustration, she walked away to another store.

Sometimes it feels like no one listens to us. We try to communicate what we mean, but it never gets through. It is frustrating when we deal with people who will not listen to what we say, and they themselves never quiet down. There is much to be said for the person who learns to listen instead of talk. When we listen, we learn. When we talk, we block learning. A fool loves to hear the sound of his own voice, but the wise person rejoices in what can be heard. We need to learn to listen, so that we can honestly help the people who come to us for our aid. If we talk, we will close people out, and they will never come back. We deal foolishly, and we present an example that we cannot be proud of. God wants us to deal with people in love, and most people need to feel like they are being heard.

PRAYER: I know that You listen to me, Lord. Teach me to listen that I might be a blessing to those whom I serve. I want to learn all I can, and it is in silence that understanding comes. Amen.

HAVEN OF SAFETY

Every word of God is pure:
he is a shield unto them that put their trust in him.
Add thou not unto his words, lest he reprove thee,
and thou be found a liar.
PROVERBS 30:5–6

The television was packed with commercials which insulted the senses and intelligence. Christmas decorations had been up since before Halloween. The radios blasted rock Christmas carols, and every time you turned around, someone had his hand out or in your pocket. If a person wasn't careful, he might just forget what Christmas was all about. Thank goodness for the church. That was one place she could go where the world couldn't cheapen Christmas. God knew that she needed a port in the storm. She needed a place where the truth of Christmas could still shine forth, and she didn't have to worry about any intrusions.

The house of God can indeed be a haven of safety from the whirl of the world. God knows that we need a place where we can feel safe and secure. We are shielded in our faith in God, and once shielded, nothing in this world can penetrate. God loves us so much, and He protects us when we need it most. He is faithful to those who come to Him seeking rest. He cradles us in His loving arms and shuts out the assaults of the world. In Him, we can know peace and tranquility beyond our wildest dreams.

PRAYER: Most holy God, be a refuge in time of trial and a constant support as I deal with the pressures of this world. I feel lost and unprotected often, and I need You to shield and strengthen my life. Amen.

THE TATTLE TRAP

Accuse not a servant unto his master,
lest he curse thee, and thou be found guilty.
PROVERBS 30:10

Timmy was sneaking through the closets looking for presents!"

Timmy's little sister stood with her hands on her hips as she ratted to Mom and Dad.

"How do you know?" asked their father.

"I saw him do it," she replied.

"And just what were you doing in our room?" he further asked.

A frightened look came across the little girl's face as she realized that by accusing her brother, she had also accused herself.

When we try to get someone else in trouble, it is rarely out of a sense of honor or duty. More often, it is a case where we cannot mind our own business. Jesus Christ told His followers to be unconcerned with the actions of others until they made sure that all of their own actions were upright and holy. His point is this: If we spend our time minding our own business, there won't be any time left over for us to stick our noses in where they don't belong. God wants to see each of us grow, but we need to be responsible for our own lives, not the lives of other people.

PRAYER: Help me to examine my life to see what my strengths and weaknesses are. I want to develop my strengths, to correct my faults, and to grow in every way possible. Amen.

GRABBING PENNIES

The horseleach hath two daughters, crying, Give, give.
There are three things that are never satisfied,
yea, four things say not, It is enough:
The grave; and the barren womb;
the earth that is not filled with water;
and the fire that saith not, It is enough.
PROVERBS 30:15–16

The store was open late on Christmas Eve. All of the clerks had been told that they had to work regular hours if they wanted to have a job after the holidays. The owner had come to them and said that they could make a killing if they could stay open late. Someone asked the owner if he didn't think he would make enough money without the few extra hours. His reply?

"There is no such thing as enough money. I will do everything I can to get every penny out of the purses and wallets of the people in this town. If I have to grab them off the street, I will do it. We stay open—am I understood?"

The man was understood probably better than he wanted to be. God knew the man immediately, and his name was Greed. There are very few things as unlovely as a glutton, someone who takes more and more and more and gives nothing back. Greed is a form of selfishness which believes that we deserve whatever we can get; therefore, we should get as much as possible. God blesses those who give, not take. The greedy have already received their reward; it is the poor and persecuted who will have their reward come to them in heaven.

PRAYER: I wish to pursue You with everything I am. Take my life and shape it into something good. I want to make You pleased with me, Father. Lead me to do what You would have me do. Amen.

SHORT SUCCESS

For three things the earth is disquieted,
and for four which it cannot bear:
For a servant when he reigneth;
and a fool when he is filled with meat;
For an odious woman when she is married;
and an handmaid that is heir to her mistress.

PROVERBS 30:21–23

I t was hard to watch. The woman had never worked a day in her life. She had messed around all through college, not learning much of anything. She had wandered around the country and had never contributed much anywhere she went. She finally came home to where her father lived, and he supported her. Now he was dead, and she was rich, and she lorded it over everyone. She acted as if this was the life she was entitled to. For people who had to slave for everything they got, it just didn't sit right.

It looks at times as though evil will triumph over good, and that injustice is the rule rather than justice. We live our lives the best way we know how, and it is a struggle. Others do nothing good, living lives of selfishness and sin, and they seem to have it all. The problem is that we see with short sight. It appears that they prosper for a good long time, and in the course of a lifetime, that is true; but when we think in terms of eternity, the evil only prosper for a short while, and we have the assurance of a life everlasting that will be full of blessings. All our trials will end, and we will find reward beyond our wildest imaginations.

PRAYER: Help me not to be jealous of the prosperity of the evil.
They will flower, then fade away, while I will blossom eternally
with the power and glory of Your love. Amen.

GOD'S CARE

There be three things which go well, yea,
four are comely in going:
A lion which is strongest among beasts,
and turneth not away for any;
A greyhound; an he goat also;
and a king, against whom there is no rising up.
PROVERBS 30:29–31

She felt safe when she was with her father. She remembered the time that the two wolves came around. He had taken his gun out and had shot them both. Everyone else in the town had been afraid, but not her father. He stood up for everything that was right and good, and if there was something that had to be done, he did it. That was just the kind of person he was. Whenever she came home, the same old feelings of safety and comort were there. As long as her father was there, everything would be just fine.

It is good to know that we are loved, and sheltered, and cared for. It is comforting to know that in this harsh and hard world, someone will stand up and not let anything happen to us. That is what faith in God is all about. When we come to know God, we realize that we are never out of His sight and that He will watch over us and protect us and care for us all the days of our lives. This assurance turns our lives from burdens into joys. He has given us the gift of life, and it is a blessed gift which He rewards time after time. His love knows no bounds, as evidenced by His greatest gift of all—the Christ, the Babe of Bethlehem.

PRAYER: My God, You are with me in all of the dark hours and hard times. I do not know what I would do without You. Thank You for being with me, Lord. Amen.

GOD WANTS TO HELP

It is not for kings,
O Lemuel, it is not for kings to drink wine;
nor for princes strong drink:
Lest they drink, and forget the law,
and pervert the judgment of any of the afflicted.
PROVERBS 31:4–5

The promotion was what he had dreamed of. He had worked all his life to get where he was, and he intended to celebrate. But the celebration had gone on too long. He found that the drinks, which had originally been intended as self-congratulation, turned into a way of dealing with pressure. As the stress built, so did his dependence on alcohol. He began drinking at the job. His performance slipped, and his work had been for nothing, thrown away by a dependence on a crippling crutch.

In our weaknesses we do foolish things. We try to find our own ways to make it through life, and we turn from the only good way there is—Jesus Christ. Christ was sent to earth to conquer death and to give people a source of strength and courage by which they could live. The gift of Christ is more powerful than anything the world can throw at us. All we need is the wisdom to see its power and to take hold of it for our lives. God will bless our lives, and He will help us through every hard time. His love for us has been proven time and again, and there is nothing on earth that will ever turn Him from us.

PRAYER: I walk dangerous paths, Father, and I am not wise enough to avoid all the pitfalls. Guide my steps with Your divine light, that I might not stumble but walk surely, bringing glory and honor to You. Amen.

A Virtuous Woman

Who can find a virtuous woman?
for her price is far above rubies.
The heart of her husband doth safely trust in her,
so that he shall have no need of spoil.
She will do him good and not evil all the days of her life.
PROVERBS 31:10–12

The trip was so long and hard. The burro kept staggering from side to side, and Mary felt as if she were going to burst. She and Joseph knew that the baby was coming soon, and they were trying desperately to find a place to rest. She never said a word of complaint. She knew that her child was to be blessed, and she trusted in God that He would protect and shelter them. She did not know why she had been selected of all women to bring God's Son into the world, but she was filled with pride and excitement.

Joseph looked upon her, and he felt glad. He was proud of Mary and he felt doubly blessed by the Lord. He was entrusted to bring up the Son of the Most High God and to care for his own lovely wife. The pair moved in to Bethlehem joyful and at peace, for they knew that God was with them.

God is with us each day. When we live our lives according to His will, then we become a blessing to those around us. Wives become blessings to husbands, and husbands to wives, children to parents, and sisters to brothers. A life well lived is a gift, not only to God and ourselves, but to everyone we meet.

PRAYER: Make my life virtuous and good. Help me to bless the lives of my family and friends. Shine Your love through my life, that I may be a beacon of Your light. Help me to glorify You in all things. Amen.

A Good Example

She girdeth her loins with strength,
and strengthenth her arms.
She perceiveth that her merchandise is good:
her candle goeth not out by night.
PROVERBS 31:17–18

She was an organizer. Everything had to be done in a particular order at a particular time. She knew she was a perfectionist, but it had always paid off. She usually got what she set her sights on, and everyone knew that she was dependable and trustworthy. If there was a job that they needed done by a specific time, they came to her. She was proud of her accomplishments, and it gave her a deep satisfaction to know that other people looked at her work to improve their own. She was an example, and she vowed that as long as she lived, she would be a good one.

In this day and age, too few people are concerned with quality and integrity. Many try to get by with exerting the least amount of effort possible, and they refuse to give more than they are asked for. It is the wise person who knows to give all he can. God is hoping that we will be bright and shining examples of truth and goodness. When we live our lives to the fullest, then we do God honor, and His glory is spread through our lives. God will bless us richly if we will only strive to be the creations He intended us to be.

PRAYER: Lord, I sometimes let down and don't do all I should to make You proud of me. Help me see ways that I can improve myself, and in doing so, bring honor and glory to You each day. Amen.

Riches of Love

She is not afraid of the snow for her household:
for all her household are clothed with scarlet.
PROVERBS 31:21

She looked back over her life, and she was satisfied. Never once had they been rich. Never once did they have more than they knew what to do with. That didn't mean they'd been poor. Her children had always had clothes to wear and shoes for their feet, and food enough to satisfy their bellies. They had all had to pitch in to make things go, but families ought to do that. Her children loved each other. Other families got tied up with gadgets and things, but hers had spent their time in love and sharing. The family would spend long hours talking and sitting around the fire. Those were the good times. Those memories were more precious than gold.

We can provide our family and friends with many things, but we have nothing greater to give than our love. If we will deal with people in love and kindness, we give them something worth more than the finest possessions. Money can't compare with a love that carries through our lives. God gives us such love. We may think that we are poor, that we don't have all the things we want, but if we have His love, then we are richer than kings and queens. Nothing compares with the love of God, and the person who knows such love will never know want.

PRAYER: Father, I adore You. You have been so good to me and have shared so much. Help me to share what You have given to me with others. Let me share the treasure which is in my heart. Amen.

STAND UNASHAMED

She looketh well to the ways of her household,
and eateth not the bread of idleness.
Her children arise up, and call her blessed;
her husband also, and he praiseth her.
Many daughters have done virtuously,
but thou excellest them all.
PROVERBS 31:27–29

E mma sat encircled by friends and family, and she was at peace. Looking around at her family, she felt that God was pleased with her. Her sons and daughters, grandsons and granddaughters, great-grandsons and great-granddaughters were all fine people who knew what it meant to love and knew what it meant to have faith. Her family had been brought up in the fear of the Lord, and it was worth it. In a world that was full of hurt and fear, her family was full of hope and love. There was a crowd of people here to celebrate with her, but most importantly, she knew God was here, too. She looked forward to meeting Him face-to-face.

When we have lived well, we can stand before God unashamed. He will look upon us, and the radiance of His face will warm and comfort us. He will tell us that we have run the race well and that we have been good and faithful servants, and all the hurts, frustrations, and disappointments of this life will fade away to nothingness. In our meeting with our Maker, we will understand fully just how wonderful the gift of life really is.

PRAYER: I look at the beauty and wonder in this world, and something deep inside tells me that I haven't seen anything yet. I look at the evil and pain in the world, and something cries out inside that I don't belong here. Be with me all of my days, Lord, and bring me at last to Your eternal glory, I pray. Amen.

Inspirational Library

Beautiful purse/pocket-size editions of Christian classics bound in flexible leatherette. These books make thoughtful gifts for everyone on your list, including yourself!

When I'm on My Knees   The highly popular collection of devotional thoughts on prayer, especially for women.
    Flexible Leatherette. $4.97

The Bible Promise Book   Over 1,000 promises from God's Word arranged by topic. What does God promise about matters like: Anger, Illness, Jealousy, Love, Money, Old Age, and Mercy? Find out in this book!
    Flexible Leatherette. $3.97

Daily Wisdom for Women   A daily devotional for women seeking biblical wisdom to apply to their lives. Scripture taken from the New American Standard Version of the Bible.
    Flexible Leatherette. $4.97

My Daily Prayer Journal   Each page is dated and features a Scripture verse and ample room for you to record your thoughts, prayers, and praises. One page for each day of the year.
    Flexible Leatherette. $4.97

Available wherever Christian books are sold.
Or order from:

Barbour Publishing, Inc.
P.O. Box 719
Uhrichsville, OH 44683
http://www.barbourbooks.com

If you order by mail, add $2.00 to your order for shipping.
Prices are subject to change without notice.